W9-BJL-078

Acclaim for
The Things You Can See Only When You Slow Down

"Wonderful . . . They read almost like haikus."
—Lakshmi Singh, NPR's *All Things Considered*

"Wise advice on how to reflect and slow down."   —*Elle*

"Leave this book on your nightstand to clear your head before bed."   —*Real Simple*

"It's just the thing for a quick hit of dharma right after you wake up or before you go to sleep."
—*Tricycle*, "Top 9 Buddhist Books of the Year"

"Loving, practical, and kind, *The Things You Can See Only When You Slow Down* is a beautiful reminder of the rewards of living wisely."
—Jack Kornfield, bestselling author of
A Path with Heart and *The Wise Heart*

"Filled with gems of wisdom, this book will lift up your heart and enliven your spirit."   —Tara Brach, bestselling author of
Radical Acceptance and *True Refuge*

"A glorious refuge—a timely, welcome escape from the pervasive trance of ordinary, relentlessly productive time."
—Wayne Muller, bestselling author of *Sabbath*
and *A Life of Being, Having, and Doing Enough*

"A book for our time—filled with universal truths, beautifully expressed and lovingly illustrated."
—Mark Williams, co-author of *Mindfulness*

PENGUIN BOOKS

The Things You Can See Only When You Slow Down

HAEMIN SUNIM is one of the most influential Zen Buddhist teachers and writers in the world. Born in South Korea, he came to the United States to study film, only to find himself pulled into the spiritual life. Educated at UC Berkeley, Harvard, and Princeton, he received formal monastic training in Korea and taught Buddhism at Hampshire College in Amherst, Massachusetts. He has more than a million followers on Twitter and Facebook and is one of *Greatist*'s 100 Most Influential People in Health and Fitness. His books—*The Things You Can See Only When You Slow Down*, which has been published in more than thirty languages, and *Love for Imperfect Things*—have sold more than four million copies and are popular as guides not only to meditation but also to overcoming the challenges of everyday life. When not traveling to share his teachings, Haemin Sunim lives in Seoul, where he founded the School of Broken Hearts, a nonprofit that offers group counseling and meditation for people experiencing challenges in life.

CHI-YOUNG KIM is the translator of the *New York Times* bestselling Korean novel *Please Look After Mom* by Kyung-sook Shin, for which she received the Man Asian Literary Prize, and the Korean contemporary classic *The Hen Who Dreamed She Could Fly* by Sun-mi Hwang. She lives in Los Angeles, California.

YOUNGCHEOL LEE is a Korean artist. His paintings have been shown in more than 150 exhibitions and are admired for their idyllic quality. You can see more of his artwork at www.namusai33.com.

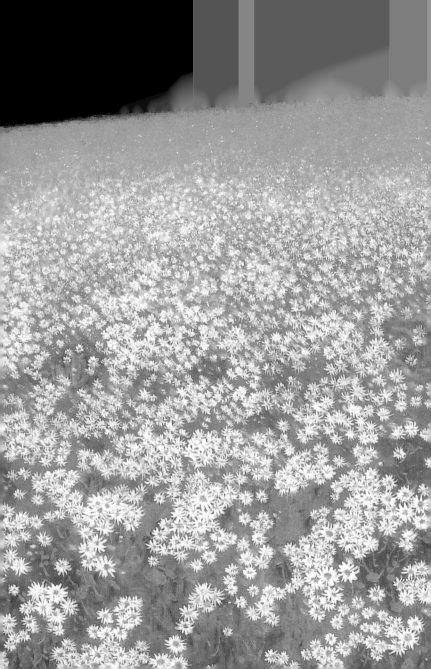

Haemin Sunim

TRANSLATED BY

Chi-Young Kim and Haemin Sunim

ARTWORK BY

Youngcheol Lee

life

The Things You Can See Only When You Slow Down

How to Be Calm in a Busy World

PENGUIN BOOKS

An imprint of Penguin Random House LLC
375 Hudson Street
New York, New York 10014
penguin.com

Published with the support of Literature Translation Institute of Korea (LTI Korea).

LIBRARY OF CONGRESS CATALOGING-IN-PUBLICATION DATA

Names: Hyemin, author.
Title: The things you can see only when you slow down : how to be calm and
mindful in a fast-paced world / Haemin Sunim ; translated by
Chi-Young Kim and Haemin Sunim ; artwork by Youngcheol Lee.
Other titles: Mæomch'umyæon, piroso poinæun kæottæul. English
Description: New York, New York : Penguin Books, an imprint of
Penguin Random House, LLC, [2017]
Identifiers: LCCN 2016036101 | ISBN 9780143130772 (hardcover)
Subjects: LCSH: Conduct of life. | Spiritual life—Buddhism.
Classification: LCC BJ1594.5.K6 H9413 2017 | DDC 294.3/44—dc23

Printed in the United States of America
13   15   17   19   20   18   16   14

Illustrations by Youngcheol Lee

Set in Centaur
DESIGNED BY KATY RIEGEL

Contents

The Things You Can See
Only When You
Slow Down

PROLOGUE

—————

As a Zen monk and former professor at a small liberal arts college in Massachusetts, I am frequently asked for advice on dealing with life's challenges. In addition to sharing my advice in person and over e-mail, a few years ago I began to answer questions over social networking sites, as I enjoyed the feeling of making connections with people. My messages were generally simple, straightforward, and short. I sometimes wrote directly in response to a real-life question, sometimes as a quick note to myself when I discovered interesting patterns of thought in mindfulness practice or in interactions with people. I also discussed the value of slowing down in our busy modern lives, as well as the art of maintaining good relationships and cultivating self-compassion.

I did not anticipate the outpouring of responses to my tweets and Facebook posts. Many people started sending me messages not only to ask advice, but also to express appreciation and gratitude. I still remember a young mother who had lost her husband in a car accident and sent me a heartfelt thank-you note for saving her from committing suicide, saying that she never thought about loving herself because love for her always meant giving it to someone else. A busy executive in his forties told me how wonderful it was to start his day with my messages; to him, they provided a moment of calm reflection and rest from his hectic schedule. A young recent graduate, discouraged after not finding a job, read my supportive words and gave the search another try, finally landing a job. When I read his news, I was overjoyed for a couple of days, as if I had gotten my first job.

It made me profoundly happy that my simple messages could inspire people and help them in their times of difficulty. As my messages came to be shared by more and more people, and my number of Twitter and Facebook followers increased, people started calling me a "healing mentor," which ended up becoming my nickname in Korea. I was then contacted by publishing companies offering to turn my writings into a book. In 2012, *The Things You Can See Only When You Slow Down* came out in South Korea; to everyone's amazement, it stayed number one on the best-seller list for forty-one weeks, and sold more than three million copies in three years. Translations followed—into Chinese, Japanese, Thai, French, and now English. I am humbled by the attention the book has received and hope it can be of help to readers of English, just as it has been to readers in Asia and France.

The book has eight chapters, addressing various aspects of life—from love and friendships to work and aspirations—and how mindfulness can help us in each. For instance, I address how to deal mindfully with negative emotions like anger and jealousy as well as life's disappointments, digging deep into my past to share my experience of failure as a new college professor. If you are overly self-conscious, the "three liberating insights"

from chapter 6 can be quite helpful. If you are anxious about your future or unsure about your true calling, I offer advice on how to increase self-awareness and how to discover it.

Each chapter opens with an essay, which is followed by a series of short messages—words of advice and wisdom addressed directly to you, to consider one by one, and to reconsider and remember, so that they may accompany you in moments of anxiety or despair, and remind you that you are not alone. Each chapter then continues with a shorter essay, followed by another series of short prompts for meditation. Throughout the book are color illustrations by Youngcheol Lee; these are intended as calming interludes, to be lingered over much like the meditation prompts are meant to be.

Some people read the whole book quickly as they would a novel. However, I would recommend that you take your time and reflect on what you have just read before moving on to a new chapter. You will enjoy it more and find deeper meanings as you go through each chapter slowly. You should feel free to make notes in the margins or highlight parts that have resonated with you.

I hope that spending time with this book becomes an occasion to reflect on and meditate in your busy life. I hope it inspires you to connect with the kinder and wiser side of yourself. May you be happy, healthy, peaceful, and always protected from harm.

CHAPTER ONE

Rest

Why Am I So Busy?

When everything around me is moving so fast, I stop and ask, "Is it the world that's busy, or is it my mind?"

WE USUALLY THINK of "mind" and "world" existing independently of each other. If someone asks where our mind is, most of us would point to either our head or our heart, but not to a tree or the sky. We perceive a clear boundary between what goes on inside our minds and what happens in the outside world. Compared to the vast world outside, the mind nestled inside the body can feel small, vulnerable, and sometimes powerless. According to the Buddha's teaching, however, the boundary between the mind and the world is actually thin, porous, and ultimately illusory. It is not that the world is objectively joyful or sad and produces a corresponding feeling in us. Rather, feelings originate with the mind projecting its subjective experience onto the world. The world isn't inherently joyful or sad; it just is.

Perhaps we can better understand this through a conversation I had with a dear friend of mine, a responsible and meticulous Buddhist nun. She recently oversaw the construction of a meditation hall in her temple. After relating the ordeal of obtaining various permits and finding the right contractor, among other things, she described the construction process in the following way:

"When it came time to place tiles on the roof, I saw tiles everywhere I went. I noticed the material they were made of, their thickness, their design. And then, when it was time to install the floor, all I could see were floors. I naturally zeroed in on the color, origin, pattern, and durability of a hardwood floor. And then it suddenly dawned on me: When we look at the outside world, we are looking at only a small part that interests us. The world we see is not the entire universe but a limited one that the mind cares about. However, *to our minds, that small world is the entire universe.* Our reality is not the infinitely stretching cosmos but the small part we choose to focus on. Reality exists because our minds exist. Without the mind, there would be no universe."

The more I reflected on this, the more her insight made sense to me. The world comes to exist because we are aware of it. We cannot live in a reality of which we are unaware. The world depends on our minds in order to exist, just as our minds depend on the world as the subject of our awareness. Put differently, our mind's awareness can be said to bring the world into being. What our mind focuses on becomes our world. Seen this way, the mind does not seem so insignificant in relation to the world out there, does it?

We neither can nor want to know every single thing that happens in the world. If we did, we would go crazy from the overload of information. If we look at the world through the lens of our mind, the way my friend did, we will readily notice what we are looking for, because our mind will focus on it. Given that the world we see through our mind's eye is limited, if we can train our mind and choose wisely where to focus, then we will be able to experience the world corresponding to the state of our mind.

As a monk and a college professor, I am pulled in many different directions. During the week I teach and conduct research, and on the weekend I drive a couple of hours to assume duties at my teacher's temple. During school breaks, my schedule becomes even busier. I need to visit senior monks, serve as an interpreter for monks who don't speak English, go to different temples to give Dharma talks, and carve out time for my own meditation practice. On top of that, I continue to research and write academic papers.

To be honest, I sometimes wonder whether a Zen monk should keep to such a full schedule. But then I realize it isn't the outside world that is a whirlwind; it is only my mind. *The world has never complained about how busy it is.* As I look deeper into myself to see why I am living such a busy life, I realize that, to a certain extent, I actually enjoy being busy. If I truly wanted to rest, I could decline invitations to teach. But I have welcomed such requests because I enjoy meeting people who want my advice and helping them with what little wisdom I have. Seeing other people happy is a deep source of joy in my life.

There is a famous Buddhist saying that everyone appears as buddhas in the eyes of the Buddha and everyone appears as pigs in the eyes of a pig. It suggests that the world is experienced according to the state of one's mind. When your mind is joyful and compassionate, the world is, too. When your mind is filled with negative thoughts, the world appears negative, too. When you feel overwhelmed and busy, remember that you are not powerless. *When your mind rests, the world also rests.*

We know the world only through the window
of our mind.
When our mind is noisy, the world is as well.
And when our mind is peaceful, the world is, too.
Knowing our minds is
just as important as trying to change the world.

*

I squeeze myself into the subway car.
People are crowded all around me.
I can either get annoyed
or think it's fun that I don't have to grab a handrail.
People react differently to the same situation.
If we look at it more closely,
we see it's not the situation that is troubling us,
but our perspective on it.

Tsunamis are frightening not just because of the water,
but also because of the objects hurled
at us by the water.
Tornadoes are terrifying not just because of the wind,
but also because of the objects uprooted and
thrown by the wind.

We feel unhappy not just because something
bad has happened,
but also because of the swirling thoughts
about what happened.

*

When you have an unpleasant feeling,
don't grab hold of it and turn it over and over.
Instead, leave it alone so it can flow.
The wave of emotion will naturally recede on its own
as long as you don't feed it by dwelling on it.

To get food unstuck from a frying pan,
just pour water in the pan and wait.
After a while the food loosens on its own.

Don't struggle to heal your wounds.
Just pour time into your heart and wait.
When your wounds are ready,
they will heal on their own.

*

If we know how to be content,
we can relax our endless striving and welcome serenity.
If we know how to be content,
we can enjoy the time we have with
the person next to us.
If we know how to be content,
we can make peace with our past and let go
of our baggage.

If you've been unable to change a bad situation, even
after many attempts,
you should change how you look at the situation.
Nothing is intrinsically good or bad.
Good or bad is always relative.
Compare your situation with someone's that is worse.
Now yours does not seem so bad after all.

*

When you are stressed out, be aware of your stress.
When you are irritated, be aware of your irritation.
When you are angry, be aware of your anger.
As soon as you become aware of these feelings
you are no longer lost in them.
Your awareness allows you to witness them from the
outside.
Awareness is inherently pure, like the open sky.
Stress, irritation, and anger can temporarily cloud the
sky,
but they can never pollute it.
Negative emotions come and go like clouds,
but the wide-open sky remains.

Like toxins slowly filling our bodies,
if anger, despair, or sorrow accumulate in our hearts,
we have to do something about it.
Exercise, talk to your mentor, meditate on loving-
kindness.
As we begin to make the effort, the toxins start to lose
their grip.

*

Do memories cause you pain?
Practice being in the present moment.
Turn your attention to the here and now.
Notice that your thoughts subside when you focus on
the present.
As your thoughts quiet, so, too, the memories.
Because memories are, in essence, thoughts.

When you leave work for the day,
if you find yourself asking,
"Do I have to live my whole life like this?"
Then try the following:
Wake up a little earlier the next morning,
and sit in silence, as if in meditation.
Breathe in deeply and slowly,
and ask yourself how your work is helping others,
regardless of how insignificantly or indirectly.
As you focus more on others,
you can reconnect with the meaning and
purpose of your work.

✳

A very modern dilemma:
There are countless television channels
but nothing interesting to watch.
Too many choices make people unhappy.

Are you feeling confused or conflicted?
Allow yourself a good night's sleep.
When you wake up the next day, the problem
will seem lighter.
It works, truly.

＊

If you would like to sleep more peacefully,
as you lay your head on your pillow,
think of the people whom you are grateful to,
or the times you helped others and felt good
about yourself.
It will warm your heart, gifting you
with more peaceful sleep.

＊

With love in our hearts,
we find even the most mundane things sacred and
beautiful.
With love in our hearts,
we become kinder and gentler, even to complete
strangers.

Without love in our hearts,
we find the world meaningless and random.
Without love in our hearts,
we become strangers even to our family and friends.

*

When we are open to others,
we dare to be vulnerable and honest.
When we have goodwill toward others,
we intend to be happy and connected.

Close your eyes, take a deep breath, and say,
"May my friends and acquaintances be loved
and protected!"
With those words, you, too, will feel loved
and protected.

When we are comfortable with ourselves
and have accepted ourselves wholly,
others will find us approachable
and will like us for who we are.

*

I wish you could see my true nature.
Beyond my body and labels,
there is a river of tenderness and vulnerability.
Beyond stereotypes and assumptions,
there is a valley of openness and authenticity.
Beyond memory and ego,
there is an ocean of awareness and compassion.

*

The wise do not fight the world.
In the most relaxed and playful manner,
they simply embody the truth that they are one with it.

When Life Disappoints, Rest a Moment

When trust is shattered, when hopes are dashed, when a loved one leaves you, before doing anything, just pause your life and rest a moment.

If you can, surround yourself with close friends and share food and drink while slowly letting out the bottled-up stories of betrayal, disappointment, and hurt.

Head to a movie theater, alone or with your best friend. Pick the silliest movie, even if you normally don't watch comedies, and laugh out loud until it hurts, and shed a few tears, as if nobody is looking, like a carefree teenager.

Find a song that speaks to your heart. Play it over and over, and sing along to it over and over, as though you are doing it for all the wounded souls.

If none of that helps, use your vacation days to take a trip. Go somewhere you've always said you wanted to go—the Grand Canyon, the Camino de Santiago, Machu Picchu.

All by yourself. Just you and the road.

After spending time alone, go to your own sacred place. Close your eyes and clear your mind.

Even if you are not that spiritual, invoke the heart of compassion and feel the embrace of acceptance.

Downcast and heartbroken, I know you were once me and I was once you.

So today, I pray for you.

Love yourself despite your imperfections.
Do you not feel compassion for yourself
as you struggle through life?
You are so eager to help your friends, but you treat
yourself so poorly.
Stroke your heart once in a while and tell yourself,
"I love you."

＊

On a piece of paper, write down everything that
stresses you out.
List everything you ought to do, including minor
things—
watering plants, replying to e-mails.
The stresses are now contained on a piece of paper,
away from your mind.
So, relax tonight.
Tell yourself you will go through the list tomorrow,
item by item, starting with the easiest.

When you open your eyes the next morning,
your mind and body will be ready.
I can guarantee that.

✻

Don't give up in the face of criticism.
Learn to brush aside what people who don't know
you have to say.
Having critics means what you're doing is
getting people's attention.
Have courage, and continue down the path you're on.

✻

Life teaches us through our mistakes.
When you make a mistake,
simply ask yourself what you were meant to learn
from it.
When we accept such lessons with humility
and gratitude,
we grow that much more.

To be happy, it's not necessary to expend great effort so
we get somewhere else.
Instead, relax into the present moment while finding
humor in your life.
With humor, life becomes light and leisurely.
And laughter always brings people to experience
openness and joy.

※

Humor opens closed hearts.
Humor can free us from the grip of our thoughts.
When we smile, we feel we can accept things we
previously could not.
We feel we can forgive those who have wronged us.
Humor is an essential part of life.

When we are joyful, our heart opens up to new things.
When we are in a bad mood, we can't be
open to new things,
no matter how wonderful they are.
Without joy in our heart,
our progress in life is slow and uninteresting.

*

Those who work in a playful, relaxed manner
tend to work efficiently and creatively.
Those who work nonstop, driven only by stress,
work without joy.

To keep doing your work for a long time,
do not treat it as just work.
View it as a source of enjoyment and growth.
The road to happiness lies not just in finding
a good job,
but also in learning to enjoy what you are asked to do.

*

Do you feel unsettled or depressed?
Then look at a child's sleeping face for one minute.
You will soon feel ripples of peace.

*

A family takes a walk amid fallen autumn leaves.
Dad lifts up his five-year-old son,
and the boy showers him with kisses.
Mom watches with a smile on her face.
If we take time to look around,
we see ourselves surrounded by lovely moments.

Would you like to make your child happy?
Then get off work a little early today.
Wait for your child in front of school.
Horse around together on the playground.
Let your child choose where to go for dinner.
And shower your child with your loving attention.
On your way home, pick up ice cream for
the family.

Your child will remember this day forever.

*

Before your children are all grown,
travel as frequently as you can as a family.
Although we see our family every day,
we don't really get to be with one another.
A change in environment can do wonders
and can bring families closer.
A good family trip can prevent divorce.

What makes music beautiful is
the distance between one note and another.
What makes speech eloquent is
the appropriate pause between words.
From time to time we should take a breath
and notice the silence between sounds.

✳

When you have to make an important decision,
don't lose sleep over it.
Just take the special medicine called "time" and wait.
Your subconscious will search for the answer.
Two days later, or three,
the answer will dawn on you
as you are waking up, taking a shower, or
talking to a friend.

Put faith in your subconscious mind and
give yourself time.

If something goes wrong,
we often turn inward and blame ourselves.
But is it really our fault?
For example, if I were James Taylor
and someone were looking for Pavarotti,
then naturally I wouldn't be chosen.
But this does not mean I lack musical talent.
It means only that I am not the right match.
So be more confident, and please stop beating yourself up.

＊

Even if you are having just a bowl of cereal for dinner,
eat it with the loving attitude of nourishing yourself.
Isn't it tiring to constantly have to care for your body?
Pat yourself on the back for the hard work
you are doing.
Then go to bed one hour earlier
as a gift to your body.

Do you have something on your mind?
Then take a walk in the sun.
Under the warmth of the sun,
your brain will release serotonin, which calms
the mind.
If you let your mind linger on the question
without trying too hard to find the solution,
an answer will emerge on its own.

＊

If you keep hoping to be comforted by others,
you can feel weighed down by that need.
If you have a constant need to be heard,
nobody can meet that need to your
complete satisfaction.
Rather than always seeking comfort from others,
offer your comfort and listen to others.
In the process of helping,
you will be healed.

Instead of a lottery ticket,
buy some flowers for yourself and your family.
If you buy flowers and place them in the living room,
you will feel like a winner every time
and find abundant beauty
whenever you pass by the living room.

*

Has something disappointed you?
Has something made you sad?
It's the school of life trying to teach you
an important lesson.
When you feel ready, take the time to
understand the lesson.

*

The world will keep turning even without you.
Let go of the idea that your way is the only way,
that you are the only one who can make it happen.

The more grateful we feel, the happier we become.
This is because gratitude helps us realize
we are all connected.
Nobody feels like an island when feeling grateful.
Gratitude awakens us to the truth of our
interdependent nature.

*

If you genuinely care for others and look for ways to
help others succeed,
you won't need to look for ways to boost your mood.
A selfless and kind act will lift your spirit
and self-worth.
If you are having a bad day, see if you can find a way to
help someone else.
Even a small gesture of help will make you feel better.

CHAPTER TWO

Mindfulness

Befriend Your Emotions

EVER SINCE I became active on Twitter and Facebook, people have been sending me messages asking for my advice. The most frequently asked question is how to deal with strong negative emotions, such as anger, hatred, and jealousy.

The good news is that those raising this question are already halfway there. The fact that they are asking the question indicates that they are mindful enough to notice the negative state of their own mind, which is not an easy thing to do. Most people are completely absorbed in their emotions and have limited self-awareness. The people who have asked me this question noticed what was happening in their minds as they were being swept into a whirlwind of negative emotions, slowed down, and then sent me a message. When people sense a negative emotion coming on, their first impulse is to control it so that they do not feel overwhelmed or threatened by it. If they can, they would like to get rid of it immediately or flee from it; they rarely think it merits deeper understanding. This is probably why people use such expressions as "managing anger" or "overcoming hatred" instead of "befriending your emotion."

It is difficult to quickly control a strong negative emotion; the more we try to control it, the more it becomes agitated and resurfaces. Even if we control it, we may end up merely suppressing it, only for it to reemerge later. Imagine that a strong negative emotion is like mud swirling inside a fish tank. To get the mud to sink to the bottom of the tank so you can have a clear view of the fish, the last thing you want to do is submerge your hands in the muddy water and try to push the mud to the bottom. The more you try to push it down, the more you churn it up. Similarly, in an attempt to control a negative emotion, you may try to push it down. Unfortunately, the harder you try, the more it resurfaces.

So what should we do? How can we better understand our negative emotions and try to resolve them instead of suppressing them? The answer is fairly simple. All we have to do is separate the raw energy of negative emotions from linguistic labels like "anger" or "hatred" and then witness it calmly until the energy morphs into something else. What is important here is not to get attached to words like "anger," "hatred," and "jealousy," and instead to witness the raw energy behind the labels. Although it may be subtle, the energy constantly changes while the label remains static. If you peel the label off and get in touch with the raw energy, you soon realize that the negative emotion is only temporary, one that changes without your efforts. Therefore, much like a mirror reflects what is before it without judgment or identification with the image, simply reflect the negative emotion—let's say it's anger—and watch dispassionately. You will see the anger slowly changing shape, either revealing a deeper layer of emotion or disappearing on its own. If another layer of emotion is revealing itself, attend to it the way you did with your anger.

When you try to understand something, it's often most effective to set aside your preconceptions and observe it quietly so that the object of your examination reveals what needs to be understood. Instead of diving into the muddy water of your emotion as a way to conquer it, you should observe it from the outside and let it settle down and transform on its own. As the spiritual teacher Jiddu Krishnamurti said, pure attention without judgment is not only the highest form of human intelligence, but also the expression of love. Observe the changing energy both attentively and lovingly as it unfolds in the space of your mind.

I can imagine someone wondering, "What is so great about just observing? Isn't it avoiding reality?" The answer is quite the opposite: You are not avoiding it; you are actually staring straight into it. Rather than getting caught in the emotion without any self-awareness, you are inquiring and then feeling what is there. As you get better at it, you will realize that the negative emotion is not a fixed reality. It naturally emerges and retreats within the space of your awareness, regardless of your will. Once you awaken to this truth, you will not be swayed by negative emotions and can regard them as a passing cloud instead of identifying with them as a defining part of your self. Do not fight your negative emotions. Observe and befriend them.

If you want revenge because your feelings are hurt,
all you can see is your own suffering.
But if you calm yourself and look more deeply,
you will see that the person who hurt you is
suffering, too.

＊

In the chambers of our heart,
we have two tenants living side by side:
Adolf Hitler and Mother Teresa.
When we are overcome by insecurity and fear,
we feel the inner workings of Hitler.
When we are in touch with love and connection,
we hear the gentle voice of Mother Teresa.

＊

We lose interest in movies or TV series
in which good characters are always good and bad ones
are always bad.
This does not match up to reality.
No person is always good or bad.

"No person can be found
Who has been, is, or will be
Only criticized
Or only praised."
—*The Dhammapada**

＊

A moral purist who is quick to judge others
often fails to see the flaws within himself.

＊

When someone criticizes another,
you might think he deserves it.
But if you look more closely,
you'll see that the critic is complaining because he did
not get his way.
So do not be so easily swayed.

---

*Gil Fronsdal, translator, *The Dhammapada: A New Translation of the Buddhist Classic with Annotations* (Boulder: Shambhala, 2011).

When you attack someone,
it is often because you are afraid.

＊

A friend starts talking ill of someone you don't like,
and you agree wholeheartedly.
But then you can't help but wonder,
"When I'm not around, does she speak ill of me too?"
Gossip can be cathartic in the moment,
but it travels fast and can bite you back.

＊

The reason you regard me as pure and compassionate
is that you are pure and compassionate yourself.

＊

When people who don't know you well admire you,
they are seeing their projected illusion,
not your real self.
In contrast, when people who know you well
respect you,
it is probably because you deserve it.

Some ask if swallowing your pride is conceding defeat.
I don't think so. Humility is a sign of
inner strength and wisdom.
When you swallow your pride, real communication
becomes possible.
We can finally hear each other and eventually
solve our problems.

✳

When someone tells you, "No,"
don't react emotionally and lose control.
"No" may open up a surprising new world to you.
"No" may unexpectedly lead you to good people.
If you begin to push back against the
unchangeable "No,"
you will suffer in the process and miss
other opportunities.

Your boss asks you to run an errand that has little to
do with your job.
Rather than getting annoyed, just do it and let it go.
Do not turn something trivial into a major
source of agony
by wasting time and energy thinking about it endlessly.

✳

If I had to summarize the entirety of most people's
lives in a few words,
it would be *endless resistance to what is.*
As we resist, we are in constant motion
trying to adjust,
and yet we still remain unhappy about what is.

If I had to summarize the entirety of an enlightened
person's life in a few words,
it would be *complete acceptance of what is.*
As we accept what is, our minds are relaxed
and composed
while the world changes rapidly around us.

Do not try to control those around you.
When you cannot control even your own mind,
what makes you think you can control others?

*

Things I liked when I was young but now couldn't care
less about:
*Airplane rides, all-you-can-eat buffets, horror movies,
staying up all night.*
Things I enjoy now that I am older:
*Mozart, brown rice, meditation, spending time alone,
regular exercise.*
We change without realizing it. We are in the
midst of change even now.

*

Do not lament that the world has changed.
Do not resent that people have changed.
Evaluating the present through the memories of the
past can cause sadness.
Whether you like it or not, change is inevitable.
Embrace and welcome it.

Whether it is an object, a thought, or a feeling,
if it has emerged out of emptiness,
it will soon change its form and
eventually retreat back to emptiness.
Seekers in search of the eternal Truth
must look beyond its impermanent nature and
become aware of "that" which *knows* impermanence.

*

The monk most venerated by other monks is not the
one who
appears most holy,
preaches the best,
runs the largest temple,
most accurately predicts the future,
has the ability to cure illness.

He is the one who teaches through his own actions.
He possesses no aura of self-importance,
and sacrifices himself first for the community.

Spirituality must be practiced
not just in solitude but also among people.
Open up to people around you and feel connected.
This is the true challenge of spiritual practice.

＊

If you are sincere about reaching enlightenment,
you can learn even from a child,
or from the person who insults you on the street.
The entire world becomes your teacher.

＊

The person leading you toward spiritual awakening
is not the one who praises you or is nice to you.
Your spirituality deepens because of those
who insult you and give you a hard time.
They are your spiritual teachers in disguise.

How can you tell if someone is truly enlightened?
Shower him with both praise and criticism.
If he shows signs of being susceptible to either,
then it means he has forgotten his enlightened nature.

*

Our emotions are capricious, like the weather
in London.
One minute, when someone criticizes us, we are
offended and furious.
The next minute, when someone praises us, we feel
proud and pompous.
Unless we recognize the still point beneath the surface
of our changing emotions,
we will feel we are hostage to their whims.

Someone advanced in spiritual practice
has the following attitude.
In a large community, she lives as though she is alone.
She minds her own business without meddling in others'.
When alone, she acts as though she is in a
large community.
She follows her regimen without sliding into laziness.

*

A great spiritual teacher can wait for her
students to mature.
She feels no need to boast of or prove her
enlightenment.
She neither imposes her teachings nor asks students to
follow her exclusively.
She lets her students be so they can grow on their own.

When a deep, honest conversation
make us feel connected to someone,
we become very happy.
The same deep connection with ourselves is possible
by wholly accepting who we are and
realizing the enlightened nature of ourselves.
This, too, is a source of incomparable happiness and
freedom.

When You Are Feeling Low

"Haemin Sunim, I'm feeling low. What should I do?"

Quietly observe the feeling without trying to change it. It will change on its own.

As if gazing at a tree in the backyard, as if sitting by a river and watching the water flow by, quietly observe your feelings as if they are external to you. If you observe your feelings in this way for just three minutes, you will notice their energy and texture slowly changing.

Feelings are often born from a matrix of conditions beyond your control. Just like you can't control the weather, or your boss's mood, you can't control the feelings in your body. They are just passing through, like clouds in the sky. They, too, dissipate on their own.

But if you take them too seriously and start internalizing them as part of your identity, then you will resuscitate them every time you think about the past. Remember that you are neither your feelings nor the story your mind tells about you to make sense of them. You are the vast silence that knows of their emergence and their disappearance.

When the mind looks outward,
it is swayed by the heavy winds of the world.
But when the mind faces inward,
we can find our center and rest in stillness.

※

People ask: "How can I clear my head when I meditate?
The more I try, the more my thoughts seem to arise."
This is completely natural—because trying to clear
your head is also a thought.

Do not try to get rid of your thoughts—it won't work.
Instead, witness the emergence of a thought.
Witness the disappearance of a thought.
The moment you become aware of it,
the mind quiets and becomes clear.

We like to talk about things external to ourselves
because our minds are accustomed to flowing out into
the world.
Spiritual practitioners, however, reverse the flow and
look inward.
They stop talking about external matters
and train themselves to become intimate
with the mind.

*

Of all the words that pour out of our mouths
every day,
how many are really ours,
and how many are borrowed from others?
How often do we say something original?
Is there such a thing as our own words anyway?

Within each of us, there is an inner witness
quietly observing what goes on inside and
outside of us.
Born from a place of silence and wisdom,
even when the world churns up a storm of emotions,
the witness sits calmly in the eye of the storm,
unharmed, luminous, and all-knowing.

※

If you wish to clear away the clouds of your thoughts,
simply keep your mind in the present.
The clouds of thought linger only in the
past or the future.
Bring your mind to the present,
and your thoughts will rest.

Rather than repeating,
"It is awful! It is awful!"
stare straight into the awful feeling.

Quietly.

Examine the feeling.
Can you see its impermanent nature?
Let the feeling leave when it says it wants to go.

＊

Everything in this universe is evanescent.
Because it is evanescent, it is also precious.
Spend this precious moment wisely and beautifully.

＊

The mind cannot have two thoughts at once.
See if you can think two thoughts at exactly
the same time.
Well? Is it possible?

We can be consumed by anger for a long time
without realizing we have been angry.
Similarly, we are easily lost in thought
without knowing we have been thinking.

Even when we are awake
we are no different from a sleepwalker.
We do things without the awareness of doing them.
Just because our eyes are open does not mean
we are awake.

＊

Being awake means that
you know what is happening within your
field of awareness.
Rather than blindly following your thoughts
and feelings,
stay awake and recognize the state of your
mind before it is too late.

When an enlightened person transcends the duality of
you and me,
she sees life as one long play.
This is why she remains humorous and lighthearted.
She plays her role but never forgets it is a performance.

*

Life is like theater. You are assigned a role.
If you don't like the role,
keep in mind that you have the power to re-create the
role you want.

CHAPTER THREE

Passion

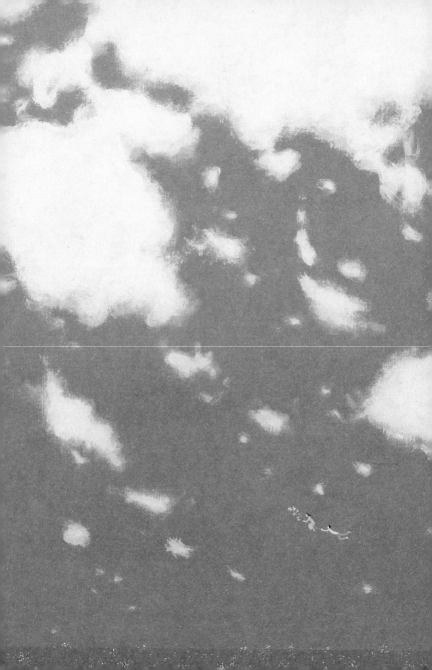

learn. To my amazement, the students noticed the difference almost immediately and began to respond positively. I didn't burden them with my overzealousness, and they slowly rediscovered their interest in the class on their own terms. When that happened, I realized something I should have known all along.

When we're first given a job, especially one we've been working toward for a long time, it's easy to become overly enthusiastic, as we are eager to prove ourselves. But in our excitement, we make the mistake of equating our own eagerness with effectiveness. Getting the job done well is more important than one's feelings of doing a good job. It takes wisdom to discern that these two are not always related. In some cases, one's zealous efforts can get in the way of achieving the desired outcome, especially if one is unable to see the needs of the others working toward it together.

Only when we know how to control this overflowing passion can we work harmoniously and effectively with others. Only then can we effectively share our enthusiasm with those around us.

The toll of a bell is heard far and wide only when the
bell is struck hard.
Your influence won't spread far without the sacrifice of
hard work.
The world notices your efforts more quickly
than you think.

*

It is important that you work hard,
but don't be enamored of the feeling of working hard.
If you are drunk on that feeling, then you care less
about the actual work
than about how you appear to others to be working
hard.

*

The most dangerous people
are those who have passion but lack wisdom.

If you want to predict how a politician will act after
winning an election,
look at how he currently lives and how he has behaved
in the past.
A person does not live the way he says he would.
He lives the way he has been living.

*

Historically, the people who bring about
change in society
tend to be not the middle-aged but
the passionate youth.
Their hearts are sensitive to the plight
of the oppressed.
Their spirits stand tall against injustice and
fight for the voiceless.
Hold on to that youthful heart and spirit no matter
how old you are.

Everyone is kind to someone they meet
for the first time.
The question is how long their kindness lasts.
Don't be fooled just because someone is nice
to you at first.

❋

When hiring, look beyond skills and experience
to see if the candidate knows how to enjoy her job.
People who enjoy their work are usually
more successful than those who don't.

No matter what we do,
the top button of our business must be fastened
properly.
If we think, "I'll just do it this way for now
and fix it later,"
it usually does not happen,
because later we may not have the motivation to fix it,
or we just get used to the way it is.

It is like moving into a house and deciding
to fix it up over time.
Even after many years, we never get around
to fixing it up.
We end up just living with the way things
are for a long time.

Someone thinks, "I'll study hard so I can get into a prestigious college."
Someone else thinks, "I'll study hard so I can teach my sister,
who cannot attend school because my family cannot afford to send her."

Although they both have the same determination to study hard,
their motivations are quite different.
A vow to help others can summon immense energy from within.
This is why people take the Bodhisattva vows to save all sentient beings
before embarking on a journey of spiritual enlightenment.

When you are making a decision, try to assess how many people it will benefit.
If it satisfies only your ego and unnecessarily hurts many, then it is the wrong decision.

✻

Be the kind of person who can put yourself in someone else's shoes
and understand something not just from your own perspective
but from theirs as well.

✻

Are you trying to get closer to someone?
Is it because you want something from him?
If you wish to be truly close, then discard your ulterior motives.
When you are genuinely kind, without an agenda, then others will more readily open up to you.

Some people are generous and kind to those outside
their circle
while neglecting the needs of those within it.
It is a mistake to take family and close colleagues for
granted.
When those closest to you feel ignored and betrayed,
everything you have built can collapse in an instant.

*

A large boulder is an example to us
of how to stay true and not to waver
even when waves of praise or criticism rush over us.

Being Right Isn't Important; Being Happy Together Is

Every one of us has beliefs, values, and thoughts that are fundamental to us and that we cannot imagine compromising on. We believe these are irrefutably right and that everyone would agree if they came to their senses. But every once in a while we have to spend time with people who do not share our convictions.

We may clash over political views, religious beliefs, or life values. If the conversation touches on these topics, it quickly becomes an argument. No one feels they are being heard or respected, and what remains is mostly anger, confusion, and hurt.

We must ask whether it was worthwhile if we make each other feel unhappy or hurt in the name of defending our beliefs. Instead of maintaining the sanctity of our values, shouldn't we care more about the person sitting in front of us? Isn't it better to be happy together than to be right alone?

Trying to convince someone to adopt our views is largely the work of our ego. Even if we turn out to be right, our ego knows no satisfaction and seeks a new argument to engage in.

Maturity comes with experience. One lesson of maturity is that we should not take our thoughts too seriously, and must learn to curb our ego and see the bigger picture.

Being right isn't nearly as important as being happy together.

Instead of being the smartest person in the room,
quick to critique others,
be the warmhearted friend, bringing people together
and sharing things.
Be the sensitive neighbor, capable of feeling
the suffering of others.

❋

If I want to convince someone,
I first listen attentively and try to understand them.
Even if I am right, they won't be convinced until they
feel heard and respected.

❋

Many conflicts in our lives can be resolved
if we put ourselves in the other person's shoes.
Try to look at things from her point of view.
If you consider only your side,
you are no different from a child.

If you get angry while debating right and wrong,
your enraged voice has just conceded defeat.

✳

Being a critic is easy.
But if the critic tries to run the operation,
he soon understands that nothing is as easy as
his criticisms.
Criticism without a solution is merely an inflation of
the critic's ego.

✳

When you hear something that makes your blood boil,
don't shoot off a text or an e-mail right away.
A wise person sleeps on it.
An instant emotional reaction often leads
to a regrettable outcome.

It is easy to make people feel special.
People usually prefer talking to listening.
Ask many open-ended questions and listen
with genuine interest.
They will feel flattered by your attention,
and even like you.

✻

A powerful person is often surrounded
by only yes-men,
helping their boss feel important and exceptional.
If the people around you always agree with you,
they are probably opportunists, not loyalists.

✻

When a question has both a long, complicated, but
logical-sounding answer
and a simple answer that can be understood
by even a child,
the right answer is usually the simple one.

When you ask a question
and there is no response,
then that is the answer.

❋

There are only those who know their shortcomings
and those who do not.
Nobody is perfect.
Everyone has shortcomings.

❋

If someone looks perfect,
then that is because you don't know
the person very well.

❋

"Don't try to make it perfect. Instead, make
it interesting!"
—AN INTERIOR DESIGNER'S ADVICE

Do you want to be happy,
or do you want to appear happy?
Never mind what the world tells you
to do to be happy.
Be truthful to yourself and discover
what you really want.

*

Choose happiness, not success, as your life's goal.
If you become successful but aren't happy, then
what is the point?

*

There are those who want to become successful
in order to thumb their noses at the people who looked
down on them.
But what happens after you achieve success?
What do you do after proving that they were wrong?
If you want to truly succeed, don't use anyone
else's yardstick.

Meaningful praise is from someone in the
same field as you.
It is worth praise from ten or more people
outside your field.

*

Professionals have their talents and areas of expertise.
If a client tries to control and monitor every detail,
the professional cannot work at full capacity
and feels inhibited.
If you want the best result, watch with interest
but know when to back off.

*

A veteran doctor, lawyer, or accountant won't
necessarily provide better service
than the passionate young professional who has been
in the field only a few years.
The amount of attention you get is often
more important
than the professional's illustrious career history.

After mastering eighteen levels of kung fu,
you can hurt someone with the flick of a finger.
But if you go on to master all thirty-six levels,
you choose to retreat when the weak foolishly
come to fight.

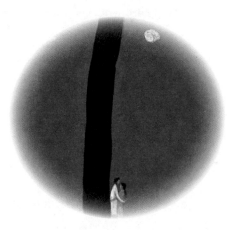

Are you moving up?

Are you doing well?

Then see whether you are succeeding

at the expense of others,

or along with others.

If you shove others aside on the way to success,

then you will be pulled under once the tide changes.

CHAPTER FOUR

Relationships

The Art of Maintaining
a Good Relationship

MANY OF US invest time and money to live in a nice house, drive a fancy car, and appear young and beautiful. But how much do we invest in the intangible, like good relationships? If we are fortunate enough to be surrounded by family and friends who love us for who we are and genuinely care for our well-being, we feel secure and emotionally stable even in the face of challenges. On the other hand, even if we possess our dream house, a luxury car, and a perfect body, we remain deeply unhappy if there are problems in our relationships. When the problems persist without any resolution in sight, we become depressed and even think of committing suicide. If happiness is what we hope to achieve in our lives, shouldn't we put more effort into cultivating good relationships with the people around us?

IN MY TWENTIES, I went on a two-week backpacking trip in Europe with a close friend from my monastery. When we arrived at the airport in Rome, our spirits were high. We had known each other for a couple of years and got along very well. I liked his sense of humor and warm-hearted nature, and he appreciated my adventurous spirit and optimism. Since he did not speak much English, I felt obligated to stay close to him. After the first seven days of spending every moment together, we'd run out of things to talk about and both became irritable. It was not because of any concrete problem in our friendship; it was just that we longed for some time alone. So the following morning I suggested we take different routes and meet up at the hostel at night. My friend welcomed my suggestion.

As I left the hostel, I felt free—I knew I could choose to do whatever I liked for the day; I did not have to negotiate with my friend about where to go first and what to see next. But as the morning turned into the afternoon, I was reminded of the advantages of traveling with a friend. When I needed to go to the restroom, I could no longer rely on my friend to watch my backpack. Eating alone was no fun; it felt more like a chore than a time for enjoyment and relaxation. I didn't take any pictures of myself that day because I did not want to bother strangers. When I encountered something beautiful, such as a famous piece of art, I was not as thrilled since there was no one to share the excitement with. When I arrived at our hostel at the end of the day, I was quite happy to see my friend. Over dinner we found many new things to talk about in recounting our respective days.

From this experience I realized that the art of maintaining a good relationship can be compared to sitting by a fireplace. If we sit too close for too long, we become hot and possibly burned. If we sit too far away, we cannot feel the warmth. Similarly, no matter how well we get along with someone, if we stick too close without building in some personal space, we soon feel trapped and burned out; it is easy to take the relationship for granted and feel resentful about not having enough privacy and independence. On the other hand, if we put in too little effort to stay in touch with friends and family, we can't feel the warmth of their love. Striking a balance is key.

I HEARD A story from Korea that holds another good lesson about relationships. It is about a man named Maeng Sa-seong (1360–1438), a member of the literati class during the Joseon Dynasty. He was renowned for his intelligence: At age nineteen he received the highest marks in the state civil service examination, and at age twenty he became county magistrate. But his quick success made him haughty and vain. One day Maeng paid a visit to an eminent Zen Buddhist master in his district and asked, "What should I keep in mind as I rule this village?"

The master answered politely, "All that is necessary is to avoid evil and to do good for many."

Maeng snapped, "Even a child knows that! Is that all you have to tell me?"

As Maeng got up to leave, the master insisted he stay a bit longer. After brewing tea, the master poured some in Maeng's cup but did not stop when the cup was full. Perplexed, Maeng demanded to know what he was doing.

"You seem to know that too much tea will ruin the floor," the master answered, "but how do you not know that too much knowledge will ruin one's character?"

Embarrassed, Maeng sprang to his feet and rushed toward the door to leave, but in his haste he hit his head on the doorframe. The master gently admonished him: "If you lower your head, you won't bump into trouble."

As we can see, too much pride can be a source of conflict. If we treat people with humility and respect, conflicts can be avoided. It is often our pride that encourages us to stand up straight and wage a battle of wills. While fighting to determine who is right and who is wrong, we end up causing physical and emotional pain. Some people even drag family and friends into the conflict and create more unnecessary confusion and ill will. If someone comes up to me and says, "Let's see whose religion is right," I first listen respectfully, then say, "Thank you for introducing me to aspects of your religion that I didn't know much about. I appreciate that." If I were to engage in an argument in order to win, the only result would be that someone would feel hurt. Even if I did win, what good would result? The other person would only feel defeated.

We all grow up in different environments. Our experiences are varied, and so are our personalities, habits, values, and thoughts. It is not easy for diverse people to live together and try to forge relationships. According to the Buddhist scripture *The Treatise on the King of Treasures Samadhi*, "Do not expect others to follow your way. When things always go your way, it is easy to become arrogant." As we experience adversity in our lives, we mature and become more understanding. Just remember that the person who has made your life difficult today could be an undercover teacher sent from above, tasked with your spiritual growth.

Do you often feel lonely at work or in school?

Perhaps your heart is closed off to those around you.

"I don't get her."

"I'm better than her."

"We're on different wavelengths."

If you think this way, how could you not be lonely?

Open your heart, and have a cup of coffee with her.

You will soon see that she is not that different from you.

*

When you open up about your hurt and sorrow,

I feel grateful that you've turned to me for support.

It's as though I am meeting you in the most sacred chamber of your heart.

Politicians always say what sounds good.
But what they say does not always resonate with us—
because their words are coming from their head, not
from their heart.

Speak from your heart, which is tender, simple,
and true.
People will understand you, and like you.

*

If you think you are either superior or inferior to
someone,
an invisible wall goes up between you.
Treat him like an old friend you haven't seen in a while.
When you let your guard down, so will he.

The end of a sushi roll, with the filling sticking out,
is often tastier than a piece sliced neatly from the middle.
Someone slick and well-put-together can come across
as cold and alienating,
while an average guy without pretense is more genuine
and attractive.

*

Do you know why that conversation is so boring?
Because we are trapped in politeness, unable to speak
from the heart.
Any conversation can become interesting and lively
as soon as we start speaking with real honesty.

When someone swears at you,
stay calm and collected for thirty seconds.
Then, that is the end of it.
But if you fight back and demand,
"What is your problem?"
you will have to spend more time with that
unhappy person.

*

People say hurtful things because they themselves
have been hurt.
When you encounter someone prickly and malicious,
think about what kind of miserable situation he must be in.
If he is too much, and you don't have time,
just whisper, "Bless you," and move on.

When you criticize someone, see if you are doing so
out of envy.
Your criticism reveals more about yourself than you
realize.
Even if you are correct, people still may find you
unappealing.

*

If you wish to communicate effectively with others,
better to describe what you are feeling rather than go
on the offensive.
For instance, say, "I am very sad to hear that,"
not, "Why do you always make me sad?"
You want people to hear you rather than have to
defend themselves from you.

When you are disappointed, don't wait
too long to say so.
When you bottle up your feelings,
the river of emotion swells,
making it difficult to cross over and speak calmly.

*

Do you have a lot of enemies?
Then be humble and stop speaking ill of people.
Those who do not make enemies are more powerful
than those who have the strength to fight them all and win.

*

The noise from a motorcycle
assaults the driver more than anyone.
The driver has only himself to blame
when he is old and can't hear anything.

When you speak ill of others,
it hurts you more than anyone—
because your negativity is loudest within you.

No matter how hurt you are, you don't need to have
the last word.
The last word can obliterate even the good memories.
Although things have changed,
is it necessary to discard all your memories,
especially the happy ones?

*

When blinded by anger, we make choices we later
regret.
Leaving the room before the bridge is burned is a
sign of maturity.

*

The best way to get even with someone
who has left you
is to meet someone new and become happy again.
Plotting for revenge and remaining jealous
after many years
is a formula for endless misery.

He complains about her behind her back.
She, without knowing anything, approaches him
and says the kindest words.
The best revenge is love.

*

Even the most beautiful music gets tiresome if I listen
to it constantly.
But if I listen to it after some time away, it becomes
wonderful again.
The problem is not the music itself. It is my
relationship with it.

Even my best friend gets annoying if I am with her for
too long.
But if I see her after a break, she is wonderful again.
The trouble is not the person. It is my relationship
with her.

There is a saying in an early Buddhist scripture:

"Paper wrapped around incense smells of incense,

and string binding fish smells of fish."

Whether we like it or not,

we naturally become influenced by our surroundings.

Ask yourself, "Who do I want to emulate?

Is that person physically or mentally nearby?"

＊

If we help someone in the hope of getting something in
return,

this is not giving but lending.

True giving is done without expecting anything in return.

It also means we relinquish control over

what we have given.

When conversation turns to someone's flaws,
try not to participate and gently redirect the conversation.
When we speak too much, it is easy to speak ill of
someone.
So when you feel talkative, just be mindful.

*

When you are asked to do something,
determine if you can do it.
If you cannot, then decline as soon as possible,
the way in a restaurant you would send back the
wrong order.
If you don't send it back immediately,
you will have to pay for it.

There is a reason people flock to certain individuals.
They are warm, nurturing, and magnanimous.
They are generous with their time, money,
and compliments.

If you try to lead people only by stressing rules and
principles,
they will leave you, one by one.
A good leader knows this, and thus tries to
cultivate virtue.

*

According to the wise Confucian scholar
Jeong Yak-yong (1762–1836):
"The best way to hide your wealth is to give it away.
If you are generous with your wealth,
the money that would have disappeared sooner or later
becomes an everlasting jewel, deeply engraved in the
heart of the recipient."

The air I inhale enters my body and becomes
part of me.
The air that I exhale moves into someone else and
becomes part of her.

Just by looking at how the air moves,
we realize we are all connected to one another,
not just figuratively but also literally.

*

"Whether we like it or not, we are all connected,
and it is unthinkable to be happy all by oneself."
—HIS HOLINESS THE DALAI LAMA*

---

*Quote from the Dalai Lama's July 11, 2011, tweet, https://twitter.com
/DalaiLama/status/90351201736065024.

The whole universe is contained in an apple
wedge in a lunch box.
Apple tree, sunlight, cloud, rain, earth, air,
farmer's sweat are all in it.
Delivery truck, gas, market, money,
cashier's smile are all in it.
Refrigerator, knife, cutting board,
mother's love are all in it.
Everything in the whole universe depends
on one another.
Now, think about what exists in you.
The whole universe is in us.

The Journey of Forgiveness

The person who betrayed you and left, the person who stole from you and disappeared, the person who stabbed you in the back and acted as if nothing happened—forgive them.

Not for them, but for your own sake—truly, completely, for yourself. Not because they deserve your forgiveness; not because they are only human.

Forgive them.

So you can be free. So you can be happy. So you can go on living your life.

It won't be easy, and it will feel unjust. A sudden gush of anger may pass through you. Tears of bitterness may roll down your face. Allow those feelings to surface, and let them be. Treat them kindly, with your compassionate heart.

After honoring your tears, ask yourself softly: "Do I want to keep carrying this resentment in my heart? Do I want to live as a victim forever?"

When you feel ready, muster your courage and make up your mind. Although your heart won't listen to your mind's decision, resolve to forgive and to free yourself from emotional bondage.

And then revisit your feelings of anger and bitterness. Give them your full permission to express themselves. How do those feelings manifest in your body? Do they become tense muscles, a rapid heartbeat, flushed skin? Do they emerge as shallow breathing, as pressure in your chest?

Let the waves of sensations surface and recede. Attend to the sensations moving through your body.

When the waves become a bit calmer, look deeply and see what is beneath them. Are there any hidden emotions beneath the anger and bitterness?

Do you see fear, shame, or grief? Is there loneliness and insecurity? Rather than drowning in them, observe them.

As your heart becomes more tender and open, turn your attention toward the aggressor. Can you look beneath that person's mask and feel what is underneath such violence and dishonesty?

Can you sense his fear, insecurity, and unworthiness? Can you feel loneliness or shame under the surface? Rather than surrendering to him, observe him compassionately.

Inside of us there is a steep mountain of fear and a deep river of grief. But there is also the compassionate eye witnessing your inner landscape. May you find your inner witness, the source of freedom and healing.

When we hate someone,
we think about him a lot.
Unable to let him go,
we gradually begin to act like him.

Don't let him become a long-term tenant of the heart.
Evict him right away with a notice of forgiveness.

*

Does the person you hate
deserve to be carried around in your heart?
Keep in your heart only those who love you.
If you carry around with you people you hate,
it causes only angst and depression.

*

In your relationships,
assume you will need to give more than you receive.
We remember so well what we have done for others
but easily forget what others have done for us.
Even if you feel you are owed a little,
it's likely you have received close to what you have given.

Seeing that I am a monk,
some people put their palms together in greeting,
and I involuntarily do the same.
Some nod,
and I involuntarily do the same.

Humans are like mirrors:
We reflect each other.

When a wise person wants something from others,
she first does what she desires from them,
exemplifying rather than asking for it.

If you want a friend to remember your birthday,
remember hers first.
If you want your husband to give you a massage,
give him a massage first.
If you want your children to watch less TV,
turn off your TV first.

Don't just wait for what you want to happen. Act first.

*

The wise man ducks his head
when someone swings at him.
If he swings back just because he was swung at,
he will be seen as the aggressor and fail to
win people's hearts.
Although it may seem unjust,
refraining from reacting out of anger shows
true character.

People turn sullen over a trivial emotional matter,
and then attack the person later
with an unrelated but logical-sounding pretext.

*

When you lower yourself, the world elevates you.
When you elevate yourself, the world lowers you.
When you arrive at the peak of enlightenment,
you will understand:
Your peak is the same height as your neighbor's.
At the peak, you see everyone's holiness.

*

When you keep clashing with someone,
it may be the world's way of asking you
to look closely at yourself.
When you don't like someone, try to figure out
what it is you don't like;
see whether you have a similar flaw within yourself.

The flaw that you immediately notice
in someone you meet
is probably a flaw of yours, too.
If you didn't have it,
you wouldn't have noticed it so quickly.

＊

No one is inherently good or bad.
Only the circumstance in which we encounter
each other is good or bad.
A criminal who happens to stop a car from running
over me
is an angel sent by God.
A Nobel Peace Prize winner who happens
to bump into me on the subway
is a jerk.

In a gathering of seven or eight people,
we will surely meet one or two who like us a lot
and one or two who are not that fond of us.
Don't take it personally; this is just
the way of the world.

*

Let people have their own opinions—
they are entitled to them.
It is when you want to change their opinion
problems arise.
This is not only impossible and futile
but also unnecessary.
How boring would the world be if everyone thought
exactly the same way?
When you grant people freedom, you will find yours, too.

*

What is the use of someone carrying a designer handbag
when her behavior lacks the same refinement?

The more you try to change your spouse,
children, or friends,
the more difficult and strained
your relationships become.
People do not change easily,
unless they suffer tremendous hardship or have
a life-altering experience.

*

I was once told by a Buddhist master that
there are two kinds of children in the world:
those born to repay the kindness of their parents,
and those born only to take what their parents have.

Ask yourself:
Which kind of a son or daughter are you to
your parents?

When you think your spouse won't change
and you worry how you will live the rest
of your life together,
ask yourself:
Am I perfect in my spouse's eyes?

❋

When faced with a problem in a relationship,
it will never be solved
if you begin by asking, "Why can't he understand me?"
or "Why won't he just do what I say?"
It is because this approach begins with a demand.

Instead, begin by asking,
"What is it that makes him unhappy and feel
misunderstood?"
or "What past experience is making him respond
in this way?"
When you begin with the intention
of understanding him,
your heart is released from the prison of your views
and opens up to feel his pain.

People who easily ignore others do so
because they are afraid of being ignored.

*

Why can't you trust that friend?
Because you know all too well
that you, too, are capable of lying
in a similar circumstance.

*

What makes us truly happy
is meeting someone who accepts us for who we are.
Even if we are successful,
we can still feel inadequate and insecure
if we are made to believe that something is
wrong with us.

According to some psychologists,
happiness can be assessed with two simple questions.
First, do you find meaning in your work?
Second, do you have good relationships with those
around you?

＊

Are you lonely because you are alone?

According to the Talmud,
every blade of grass has an angel who protects it.
The angels whisper to each blade,
"Grow! Grow!"

If even a blade of grass has an angel,
wouldn't each of us as well?
If you feel lonely,
think of the angel on your shoulder
and be grateful that you are cared for.

A mosquito has been in my room for the last two days,
and it still hasn't bitten me.
Okay, let us live together.
We must share some karmic affinity.

*

We live among countless relations:
family, friends, colleagues, neighbors, etc.
Life is good when these relationships are good.
Being happy by yourself doesn't last long.

*

For spiritual practitioners,
relationships are the final test.
Even if you have awakened to your enlightened nature,
there is still further to go in your spiritual journey
if you're not living harmoniously with others.

CHAPTER FIVE

Love

First Love

Between us, Mary, there stands an unknown god.
—KAHLIL GIBRAN*

I WAS IN tenth grade when I first came across Kahlil Gibran's books. I dove into his words without knowing who he was or where he was from. I had not yet tasted the sweetness of love or the bitterness of life, but his love poems and spiritual prose enthralled me. It was probably his poems that first put me in touch with something ineffably beautiful and sacred within myself. As I read *The Prophet* and *Jesus the Son of Man*, I felt a deep sense of reverence for, and intimacy with, Jesus. This was a new experience for me, as I had previously been

---

*Virginia Hilu, editor and arranger, *Beloved Prophet: The Love Letters of Kahlil Gibran and Mary Haskell and Her Private Journal* (New York: Alfred A. Knopf, 1972).

exposed only to dry, moralistic Christian teachings of good and evil.

Even more fascinating were the love letters between Gibran and Mary Haskell, his close friend and spiritual partner. The letters upended my inexperienced teenage heart longing for true love. I ended the many long nights of my high school years reading Gibran's poetry. I still remember how Gibran described his love in this following simple, yet elegant, sentence:

Demonstrations of love are small, compared with the great thing that is hidden behind them.*

Gibran's tender spirit and his language moved me deeply. Even though I had never fallen in love, his words dug into my heart as if I were experiencing it myself.

When love beckons to you, follow him,
Though his ways are hard and steep.

---

*Kahlil Gibran, *The Prophet* (New York: Alfred A. Knopf, 1967).

And when his wings enfold you, yield to him,
*Though the sword hidden among his pinions may wound you.**

I promised myself that when love found me, I, too, would pour all of myself into it, without calculation or fear, even if deep pain lurked behind it. But, as everyone knows, love does not arrive just because you want it to, or think you are ready for it. In fact, elusiveness seems to be the nature of love: The harder you try to grasp it, the further away it remains.

A few years later I woke up one morning and realized that my long-awaited love had finally found me. It was like an unexpected guest walking straight into my heart, regardless of my will or readiness. It is embarrassing for a monk to talk about his first love, but she was an American missionary whom I met by chance on the streets of Seoul. I was interested in religion and spirituality, so we had a lot to talk about. She taught English to me and my friends, and we helped her learn Korean. Although she was several years older than I was, we shared several interests beyond religion and languages. We both liked

---

*Gibran, *The Prophet.*

George Winston's music, Luc Besson's films, and musicals like *Les Misérables*. I made her mixtapes, and she baked me cookies and pies. Even though I rarely had a chance to be with her one-on-one, I looked forward to seeing her, even if it was in a class setting. Soon I realized this was not just a youthful crush; it was love.

But could this love come to fruition? It was fated to be one-sided. In her eyes I was just a high school student. She was due to return to the U.S. after six months, back to her longtime boyfriend. It was clearly not going to work out, but I could not do anything about how I felt. When love finds you, it consumes you; everything else becomes unimportant. My thoughts were circling her all day long, and my heart was wide open and vulnerable. Everything looked more vivid and meaningful. I felt so happy when I thought about her, as if I were flying to the highest peak in the world with her. But as the date for her to return home approached, I also felt unbearable sorrow. I was so very happy, and at the same time in acute pain.

Two weeks before her departure for the U.S., I felt my selfishness gradually dissipate. Nothing was important other than her. It was like I was disappearing from the world, leaving only her in it—as though everything in the world sprang from her. That was when I finally understood what Gibran meant when he said there was an unknown god between him and Mary. Love seemed so sacred and mysterious, like the work of a god far more powerful and significant than either of us. All of Gibran's words took on new meaning. The whole world appeared quite different to me.

Three years after she left Korea, she wrote to me to announce her wedding: She would finally be marrying her boyfriend. At that point I was in college, in California; I wanted to fly to the South to congratulate her. But I had neither the money nor the time. What really stopped me from attending her wedding, though, was the fear that seeing her get married would be too painful. I could only send a letter wishing her the best, along with a small present. Two years later I graduated from college and decided to drive cross-country with a friend. When we passed through her town, I called and asked if she would like to have coffee with me. She was thrilled to see me, and we reminisced about our time together in Korea. Her husband came with her and treated me warmly. He was a kindhearted person, just like her.

AFTER COLLEGE I lived in Cambridge, Massachusetts, where I was studying for my master's degree. I frequently visited Boston's South End, where Gibran's family lived after emigrating from Lebanon at the end of the nineteenth century—when the South End was one of the largest slums in Boston, populated largely by Syrian and Lebanese immigrants. Today, though, it's a beautiful neighborhood, with New England red-brick buildings. Gibran grew up there, living with his mother and siblings and learning English at school. He enrolled in art

school and blossomed into a talented artist. In 1904 he had his first exhibition, and Mary Haskell, who was ten years older, was taken with his artistry; she became his patron for the rest of his life. Gibran sent her letters filled with insights about love and life, and those letters, having nestled deep in my teenage heart, remain with me even today.

And when he speaks to you, believe in him,
Though his voice may shatter your dreams as the north wind
lays waste the garden.
For even as love crowns you, so shall he crucify you.*

Haskell eventually left Boston and moved to the South. Three years later she wrote to Gibran to inform him that she was to be married—just as my first love announced to me three years after her move to the South. Having this in common with Gibran made me feel closer to him, and his writings felt even more special to me. Today, when I think about my first love, I no

---

*Gibran, *The Prophet*.

longer feel sorrow. At the time, though, my heart ached. Those feelings are long gone, replaced with a deep gratitude. I am so grateful to my first love, to Gibran, and to the universe for introducing me to the wonder of love and devotion and to the feeling of being truly alive, and for giving me the experience of a vanishing ego, a universe of infinite meanings, and a glimpse of God.

If you look for love, in pursuit of what it can give you,
it will hide itself.
If you ask love to arrive because you are now ready,
it will skip your door.

Love is like an uninvited guest.
Love will come when it wants to.
Love will leave when you ask more of it.

*

If you attempt to find a love that meets certain criteria,
your new love may also make certain demands of you.
Drop your demands quickly when love knocks on your
door.

*

Love is warm and freeing.
It is innocent, like a child
without a hidden agenda.

We can determine how close we are to
someone by asking,
"Can I act like a little kid in front of that person?"
When we love someone, we feel like a little kid in our
heart.

✳

When I began looking for my first teaching job,
I thought it was similar to going out on a date.
I might like it, but it might not like me.
Or it might like me, but I might not like it.

✳

To cook something delicious,
you need time for the ingredients to marinate.
To build a lasting relationship,
you need time for trust to develop.

When you are dating, temper your enthusiasm.
You may ask, "What is wrong with expressing
my honest feelings?
Why can't I give her a gift and tell her I love her?"
Your words and gifts will mean more to her
when she is ready.
Love her, not your feelings.

✳

Love needs to be balanced.
If you like him more than he likes you,
give him time and space to catch up.
It is important to hold back your emotions
when your feelings are not in balance with his.

✳

"Haemin Sunim, I found myself getting
so upset with him.
At first I thought it was because I did not like him.
But then I realized it was because
he was not interested in me."
Anger for no reason could be the expression of a crush.

In elementary school
I met a tall girl who made fun of me.
Later I learned she was doing it to get my attention.
That was my first insight into the complexities of
human psychology.

＊

One of the worst feelings is to believe
that you don't matter.
Look around you.
Have you intentionally or unintentionally
ignored anyone?

＊

Only when we are hurt
do we think of someone
whom we have hurt
and feel true remorse.

The end of a relationship reveals what we are made of.
Move away, just one step, from your stubbornness
and anger.
That one step is more significant than ten steps
when things are fine.
It will diminish your pain and rescue
you from insanity.

*

The heart is slower than the mind.
The mind knows you must part ways,
but your heart does not.
This is because your feelings are settled deeper
in your heart.

When one day, after many days of disappointment,
your partner deals the final blow,
the light finally dims in your heart.

Fallen gingko nuts are like a failed relationship.
Once so lovely hanging from the tree,
they emit a stink as they are crushed underfoot.
Be as gentle in ending a relationship
as you were in starting it.

*

Proof of having really loved:
You do not speak ill of your ex
even after your relationship has ended.

*

Sometimes, after a relationship is over,
you catch yourself thinking,
"I hope she is happy," without bitterness.
This is a sign you have moved on.

Pain caused by one person can be healed by another.
But before you go out to meet someone new,
make sure to give yourself time to be whole again.
Otherwise you may end up using the new person you meet.

*

An exceptional relationship is not
one with a good beginning
but one with a good ending.
Relationships often begin accidentally,
but when it comes to ending them,
we usually have choices.
Choose the ending wisely.

I Love Your Ordinariness

After my Dharma talk, you approached me shyly, with a warm bottle of soy milk in your hands, and said tenderly, "Sunim, I am sorry I can only afford to offer you this." After handing me the bottle and a note, you disappeared into the crowd.

When I read your note, I was deeply touched: "Thank you from the bottom of my heart for listening to me and offering your advice to such an unremarkable, ordinary person like me."

With the warmth of the bottle still lingering in my hands, I regretted that I missed the opportunity to speak with you further. Since we may not meet again, I decided to write to you here, hoping this message might somehow reach you.

I want you to know that I love your ordinariness, because I, too, am ordinary. The truth is, we are all ordinary.

No matter how famous or beautiful one is, no matter how much money or power one has, no matter how many wonderful accomplishments one has had, we all have our share of setbacks, heartbreak, and loss. We have to face challenges we have no control over. Loneliness and the fear of death will accompany us to our final days. Everyone is on the same treacherous journey of life's tainted glory.

So I love you, you who shyly stood before me, murmuring softly that you are ordinary, offering the warm bottle of your heart.

Without love,

our lives would pass us by

in the blink of an eye.

Love has the power to stop the world for a moment.

✳

Love makes the world look beautiful.

When there is love, there is beauty.

When love is drying up in your life,

look for the beauty around you.

That is where love can be found.

✳

You are beautiful

not because you are better than others

but because there is only you who can smile like that.

May you fall in love with your unique self.

One summer night, I look up and focus on one star
out of many.
That star also chooses to look at me, out of all the
people on earth.
A meeting between two people is like this,
a rare cosmic event.
It is one in a million, a billion, a trillion.

*

Love is
trusting someone,
being there for someone,
being ready to listen with a tender heart
for no other reason than love.

At times we are not sure
whether what we feel is love.
At that moment, ask yourself this:
"Am I happy to give more even after having given a lot?"
If the answer is yes, and there is no regret afterward,
then that is probably love.

✻

Love means loving someone the way she is.
Wanting her to be a certain way is not love
but your desire.
Do not attempt to improve someone in the
name of love.
It is improvement only in your eyes, not in hers.

If something is meant to blossom into a relationship,
it usually works out without much difficulty.
If you are the only one putting in effort,
then let him go.
This may relieve the pressure, and motivate him to
make effort.
If not, then it will open up a new path for you.

*

Love comes naturally and effortlessly.
If you try to love someone, then it is not real until you
stop trying.

*

A casting director auditions many actors
but recognizes the right one as soon as he walks in.
It can be the same with a new house, a diamond ring, a
future spouse.
If you are hesitant, then you might not have found the
right one yet.

Love her
without "What if,"
without calculation,
without second-guessing,
without comparing her to others.

Love her with the steadfast conviction of your soul.
If one of you is unshakable, then the relationship
can last.

*

Please don't call it love.
What you are experiencing is infatuation
with no commitment or responsibility.

Infatuation is not love
because it begins and ends with you.
It is more about your feelings, and less about the other
person.

*

When we are in love, we like to do nice things for the
one we love.
But it is equally important to refrain from doing
unnecessary things.
We often overlook that part.

We like to get involved in other people's business,
thinking we are doing so for them.
We offer unsolicited help and interfere with their lives.
We take away their power and make them
feel incapable.
This stems from our desire for control
and recognition.
It has little to do with love.

∗

We should love people like the sun loves the earth.
The sun loves the earth without choosing to.
It nourishes trees and flowers, expecting
nothing in return.
It does not withhold its rays but brightens everything
with its presence.

Like Kahlil Gibran said,

love each other like

two pillars supporting the same roof.

While looking out on the horizon together,

allow space between you and your loved one.

Without it, you will suffocate and exhaust your love.

✻

Remember this:

When you struggle to hold on to her, she leaves.

When you decide to let her go, she stays.

✻

We do things for the one we love,

but sometimes just being there expresses even

deeper love.

Give the gift of your full presence.

CHAPTER SIX

Life

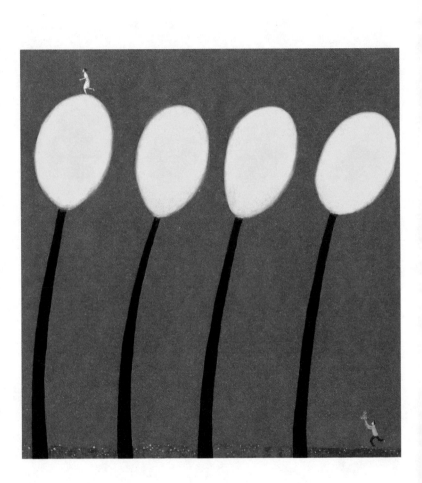

Do You Know Kung Fu?

WHEN I WALK around New York City in my gray monastic robes, I often encounter little boys who imitate Bruce Lee upon seeing me. At first I didn't understand what they were doing, but soon enough I did—they assumed anyone with a shaved head, wearing robes, would know martial arts. I thought this was cute and amusing. A more forward boy even asked me if I knew kung fu like those Chinese monks at Shaolin Temple. The playful side of me wanted to make a few fake kung fu poses, slowly raising my arms and my right leg.

When adults find out that I am a Buddhist monastic, they ask with curiosity, "What kind of meditation do you practice?" or "How many hours do you sit every morning? Your mind must be very peaceful." Then they talk about their experiences at a local Zen center or yoga studio, or tell me about a book on mindfulness they have come across. For many adults in the West, it seems that a Buddhist teacher is someone who is serene and collected thanks to daily meditation. Although the assumptions of the child and the adult are different, I find that there is an underlying similarity. Both child and adult are curious about what it is that a monk does. In other words, when it comes to imagining a monk's identity, people in the West tend to zero in on his behavior.

When I am in Korea, a different set of questions awaits me. On the subway, for instance, the person sitting next to me might ask, "Where is your home monastery?" or "Which temple do you currently reside in?" For Koreans it appears that the most defining part of a person is where he lives. Even in the U.S., when Koreans first meet, after exchanging names the first question they ask is, "Where in Korea are you from?" It seems that for many Koreans, one's identity is tied closely to his hometown rather than to what he is doing.

Every time I return to Korea, I wonder why Koreans are so obsessed with their alma mater, even when they are over fifty years old. Of course, when it comes to finding a job, having graduated from a prestigious university is advantageous in most parts of the world. But the degree alone is often not enough. Even if one has landed a good job, one's skills and experience are more important than where one has studied. A good example is Steve Jobs, the cofounder of Apple. Jobs went to Reed College but dropped out after one semester. Anyone familiar with American higher education would know that Reed is an excellent liberal arts college in Portland, Oregon. But to an average Korean, who has heard only of the Ivy League and a few large universities in California, Reed would be considered subpar. If Steve Jobs had been Korean, his educational background would have been a huge impediment to a successful career. Nobody would have taken his ideas seriously or invested in his company; he would have been seen as not smart enough to have gone to an Ivy.

This concerns me. If we consider someone's identity as rooted primarily in his hometown or the school he graduated from, we end up looking only at his past and not paying attention to his current skills or future vision. Only those born into good families with the right educational background and connections are given a chance to succeed, while those from less-than-ideal backgrounds who are brimming with potential are denied opportunities.

Whenever young boys approach me to ask if I know kung fu, it becomes an occasion for me to reflect on my life. Am I behaving like a spiritual teacher? Or have I become complacent in my identity and ignored the work I am called to do? Moreover, when I meet someone new, do I make an effort to see who he is beneath his social markers? Or am I reducing people to their background and failing to see who they really are? I am reminded again that anyone, including those young boys, can be our spiritual teacher if we are willing to open our hearts to them.

Life is like a slice of pizza.

It looks delicious in an advertisement,

but when we actually have it, it is not as good as we

imagined.

If you envy someone's life,

remember the pizza in the ad.

It always looks better than it is.

*

Have you ever selected a cheaper dish from a menu

than the one you really wanted,

only to regret your choice when it arrived?

Always go with your first choice if you can afford it.

It is better than a life filled with regrets.

There are many more ordinary hours in life than extraordinary ones.
We wait in line at the supermarket.
We spend hours commuting to work.
We water our plants and feed our pets.
Happiness means finding a moment of joy in those ordinary hours.

✻

When you concentrate, even a phone book can be interesting.
If you are bored, maybe you are not concentrating.

✻

Wherever you go, cultivate a sense of ownership.
If you see litter in a church, library, or park, pick it up.
As you take ownership, your life will have more purpose,
and people will notice your good example.

It makes sense that Scandinavia should be famous
for furniture design,
since people in a cold climate spend more time inside
their homes.
Similarly, Italy is renowned for designer apparel;
it makes sense that people in a warm climate
should pay more attention to how they appear outdoors.

Where you live shapes you.
Do you live in a place conducive to
the pursuit of your dreams?

*

We don't think twice about spending
nine or ten dollars on a glass of wine.
And yet we hesitate when it comes to buying a book,
which is the price of only one or two glasses of wine.

Apparently most people are unable to tell the difference between a $15 bottle of wine and a $50 bottle.
The extra $35 is the price of our vanity.

*

When purchasing something you will have for a long time, like a house or a piano,
choose the best within your means, not something that will do for now.
You might think it is good enough, but after a while you will regret it.

*

A good customer does not say, "Please do whatever you think is best."
She knows exactly what she wants and communicates it clearly.
If a customer does not communicate what she wants, she may still have preferences,
which might be expressed as a complaint once the work is completed.

When there is a problem,
take it up with the person who is responsible.
If you address it in a roundabout way,
through other people,
out of fear of upsetting the person and your relationship,
then the problem becomes more complicated.
Go straight to the source and deal with the person directly,
even if this makes you uncomfortable.

*

The more you know,
the more you think you don't.
The more you don't know,
the more you think you do.

Any social phenomenon is difficult to generalize.
Its causes are embedded in a complex web of history,
culture, politics, and economics.
If someone explains a social phenomenon
in simple terms,
he is either an expert or a fool.

*

The biggest obstacle to learning
is pretending to know even when you don't.
It is better to admit you don't know something;
if you pretend, you have to act as if you knew all along.
It is easier to learn when you set aside your pride and
are honest.

*

The compassionate gaze of the wounded soul is
more beautiful than the naive smile of the
inexperienced youth.

The determination to convince someone might stem
from being
not completely convinced yourself.
I do not go around trying to convince people that
I am a man.

✳

Wear confidence.
It is the height of fashion.

✳

When we hold too firmly to our beliefs,
we risk being blind to reality
and seeing only what conforms to our beliefs.

✳

The person who says,
"That person is so political,"
is usually just as political, if not more.

Admiration does not come easily.
Rather than setting a goal of becoming rich
and powerful,
aim higher: becoming admired in your field.

*

One of the greatest blessings in life is meeting someone
we truly admire.
That person becomes a beacon of hope, shielding us
from cynicism.

*

Sometimes life throws us a curveball
for no reason that we can fathom.
But do not despair.
We are not alone. We can persevere.
This, too, shall pass, like the heat of summer.

As you enter your forties, you start to think:
"Is this what life is all about? Is this all there is?"
That sad and hollow feeling—I, too, know it.

*

Love,
not righteous words,
can change people's lives.

Three Liberating Insights

One spring day as I turned thirty, I looked into my mind and realized three things. The moment I realized them, I knew what I had to do to be happy.

First, people are not as interested in me as I had always believed. I cannot remember what my friend was wearing when I saw her a week ago. Or how her makeup was or what her hair was like. If I cannot remember, then why would she remember similar things about me? Although we do think about others from time to time, it is rarely for more than a few minutes. When we are done thinking about other people, our minds revert to what immediately concerns us. Why should we spend so many hours of our lives worrying about how we appear to others?

Second, not everyone has to like me. After all, I do not like everyone. Certainly for all of us, there are politicians, coworkers, clients, and family members we simply cannot stand. So then why should everyone like me? There is no need to torment yourself because someone dislikes you. Accept it as a fact of life; you cannot control how others feel about you. If someone does not like you, let her have her opinion. Just move on.

Third, if we are brutally honest with ourselves, most things we do for others are in fact for ourselves. We pray for the well-being of our family because we need them to be around. We shed tears when our partner dies because of the impending loneliness. We sacrifice for our children in the hope that they will grow up the way we want. Unless we become enlightened like the Buddha or Jesus, it is difficult to abandon our deep-rooted preoccupation with ourselves.

Stop worrying about what others think and just do what your heart wishes. Do not crowd your mind with "what ifs." Uncomplicate your life and own up to your desires. Only when you are happy can you help to make the world a happier place.

Do not let people's opinions of you determine
who you are.
Instead of worrying about what others think,
devote yourself to your dreams.

✻

When someone does not like us,
it is not our problem but theirs.
Not everyone will like us.
This is a problem only if we let it bother us.

✻

By complaining that something we have to do is
too hard,
we add another layer of difficulty.
Take a deep breath, and then just do it.

Write down on a sheet of paper
the names of the places you want to travel to before
you die,
the people you hope to meet,
the concerts you know you will enjoy,
the sports games you are dying to see,
the restaurants you have to try.

Then experience everything on the list, item by item.
Nobody needs to know about the list.
Allow yourself a little secret of your own.
It will feel good to do something just for yourself.

*

Life is like jazz.
Much of it is improvised; we cannot control all the
variables.
We must live it with panache and flair,
regardless of what it throws at us.

We can love our family and pray for their happiness.
We can give advice and help when needed.
But we can neither make decisions for them
nor make them act the way we want them to.
There are many things we cannot control in life.
That includes those closest to us.

*

If you learn to play one sport well, it becomes easier
to learn to play another.
If you become fluent in one foreign language, you can
more easily learn another.
If you figure out how to run a small business, it'll be
easier to run a second or third one.
Do not be envious of those who are good
at many things.
First learn to be good at one. You will soon be able
to do two or three.

A majestic tree is the first to be cut down
and used for lumber,
whereas a modest one lives on.
Likewise, a real master conceals his virtue and never
boasts of his excellence.

*

Dream big but start small.
A small adjustment can have a big effect on your life.

For example, if you want to be healthier,
then start by going to bed a half hour earlier.
If you want to lose weight,
then start by drinking water instead of soda.
If you have an important project to complete,
then start by getting your desk organized.

"Keep your thoughts positive, because your thoughts become your words.

Keep your words positive, because your words become your behavior.

Keep your behavior positive, because your behavior becomes your habits.

Keep your habits positive, because your habits become your values.

Keep your values positive, because your values become your destiny."

—MAHATMA GANDHI*

*

Your mind cannot hold two thoughts at once.

This means that a single thought can occupy your entire mind.

Whether good or bad, everything stems from a single thought.

If we are careful with that first thought, even tragedies can be prevented.

---

*Taro Gold, *Open Your Mind, Open Your Life: A Book of Eastern Wisdom* (Kansas City, MO: Andrews McMeel, 2002).

We prefer the right words to the wrong words.
We prefer honest words to the right words.
We prefer real acts to honest words.

How you speak is often more important than
what you say.
And actions speak louder than words.

＊

Knowledge wants to talk.
Wisdom wants to listen.

A foolish person thinks, "I already know that."
He keeps anything new from coming into his mind.
A wise person thinks, "I don't know the whole story."
She opens herself up to even greater wisdom.

✻

An ordinary person mainly notices particular things he
likes or dislikes.
A wise person notices both the whole
and the particulars.

✻

When you share your problems with your friends,
you do not expect them to have the solutions.
You are just grateful they are there for you
and willing to listen.

If someone shares his problems with you,
don't feel the need to have the solutions.
Just listen sincerely. This is often more helpful.

When I look deeply within myself,
I realize what it is that I really want from others:
attentive ears that listen to what I am saying,
kind words that acknowledge my existence and worth,
gentle eyes that accept my flaws and insecurities.

I resolve to be that person for those around me.

*

A bad driver brakes often.
A bad conversationalist also brakes often—
interrupting the flow with his own stories.

*

You can fool someone for a moment,
but it is hard to fool someone for long.
Time will tell if someone has spoken from the heart
or made things up to get what he wanted.
Even if he got what he wanted with a momentary lie,
the fact that he lied will stay with him
until the day he dies.

When there is no envy or expectation,
even the wealthiest and most powerful person is just
another human being.
Only when we are envious of what he has, or expect
something from him,
do we become discontented and lose our composure.

*

Swindlers love to sweet-talk about future gains,
insisting that things will work out if we listen to them.
When our greed is awakened, we are cheated.

*

A clever negotiator leads the other party to think
they've won
while getting everything he wants.
If the other party feels flattered and superior
and lets the clever negotiator have his way,
then it is really the negotiator who has won.

A cruel irony:
The reward for someone who works hard is more work.

*

If we're quick to grant a favor, then people quickly
forget their gratitude.
If we grant a favor with several conditions, then people
express immense gratitude.

CHAPTER SEVEN

The Future

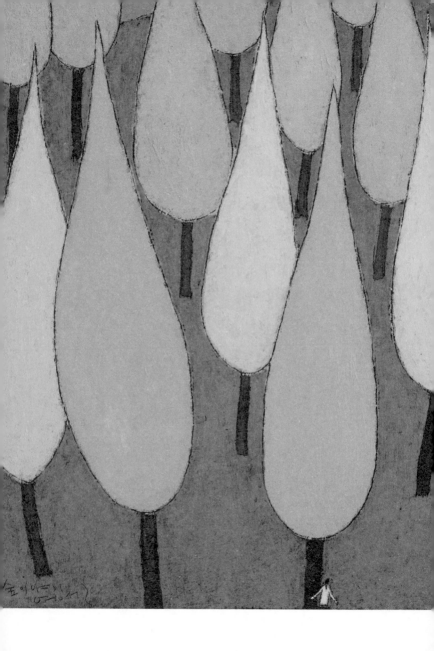

One Word of Encouragement Can Change the Future

UNLIKE IN CHRISTIANITY, there are many thousands of scriptures in the Buddhist tradition. Some are highly philosophical; others are mainly stories that contain important life lessons. My favorite is the Lotus Sutra, which has both philosophical teachings and didactic narratives. Like with any sacred text, the more I study it, the more I am awed by its depth.

As I was reading the Lotus Sutra again recently, one chapter in particular, "Prophesy of Enlightenment for Five Hundred Disciples," caught my attention. It describes the Buddha giving a prophesy of complete enlightenment to his five hundred disciples, telling them that they will all become Buddhas after a certain period of time. A prophesy of enlightenment is the Buddha's guarantee as well as his prediction of when and at what point his disciples will reach the final stage of buddhahood. Hearing the Buddha's encouraging words about their future, the five hundred disciples are elated and make a vow to engage continuously in spiritual practice. Whenever I come across this story of the Buddha's prophesy, it reminds me of my elementary school teacher Ms. Lee, who predicted great things about my future.

By all measures, I was just an average kid. I was of average height and came from a middle-class family. I was not the brightest student, but neither was I a troublemaker. I remember Ms. Lee as a strict woman in her mid-thirties. She had one son who attended the same school; I knew him quite well because we had been in the same class the previous year. One day, as I was walking across the yard after school, Ms. Lee's son came up to me and invited me over to play at his house—he said his parents had bought him some new toys. I was very much tempted but was afraid I might run into Ms. Lee. Understanding my hesitation, my friend assured me that his mom rarely came home before four o'clock.

I agreed to play with him only if I could leave before four o'clock.

We had a lot of fun playing with his new toys. I became absorbed in playing and completely forgot about the time when the front door swung open and my teacher walked in. I tensed up, worried that I would be chastised for playing instead of doing my homework. To my surprise, Ms. Lee greeted me with a big smile. She spoke to me warmly and gave me a hug as though I were her son. In her embrace, I realized she was actually a kind and loving person, but she had no choice but to appear strict at school because she had to maintain control over the class. She gave me a snack that she gave my friend only on special occasions. As I ate it, she stroked my head gently and said, "You're going to be a good student and a role model for your friends. I trust that you will become a great person who brings wisdom and happiness to a lot of people."

My young heart was moved beyond words. After that day, I studied very hard and tried to be a role model for the other students. Since Ms. Lee had put her trust in me, I was determined not to disappoint her. I think

I have become who I am today thanks to what she said to me that afternoon. Without her kind words, I would not have had the confidence to excel academically or to become a professor or spiritual teacher.

According to the Lotus Sutra, the Buddha makes the prophesy about his disciples because he has a supernatural ability to foresee when they would achieve the final stage of buddhahood. But I do not think they automatically attained enlightenment because they received the Buddha's prophesy; I think it had a lot to do with the Buddha's faith in them, which motivated them to work harder to accomplish what their teacher predicted. Like Ms. Lee's words to me, the Buddha's trusting words and his loving gaze transformed the lives of his five hundred disciples. One word of encouragement, said with kindness and hope, can change a person's future, the way it did for the five hundred disciples and for me.

Some say they don't really know what they are looking
for in life.
This might be because, instead of getting in touch with
how they feel,
they have led their lives according to other people's
expectations.
Live your life not to satisfy others, but to fulfill what
your heart desires.

*

My dear young friend,
please don't feel discouraged
just because you are slightly behind.
Life isn't a hundred-meter race against your friends,
but a lifelong marathon against yourself.
Rather than focusing on getting ahead of your friends,
first try to discover your unique color.

"Haemin Sunim, I hope you become a great teacher like the Dalai Lama."
"Thank you for your kindness. I deeply admire His Holiness.
But I don't want to become the Dalai Lama.
I would like to become Haemin Sunim."

＊

Don't flit here and there like a school of fish
just because that is what your friends do
or because others say it is what you should do.
Stand by your convictions.
Upend the existing paradigm
and become a trendsetter.

There are things I would have liked to teach my child
if I'd had one:
No matter how famous, powerful,
or rich some people are,
they are not very different from anyone else.

We long for deep connection and unconditional
acceptance.
We have the same insecurities and need for approval.
There is no reason to feel inferior.

*

If you are raising a child, then remember this:
It is okay for your child to do well in one area
and not so well in others.

A restaurant specializing in a few good dishes
is more likely to develop a good reputation
than one with a lengthy menu.
Help your child go deep in her area of interest.

Intelligence is not just about getting straight A's and
high SAT scores.
It is also about being able to empathize and be attuned
to how other people feel.

*

Are you a controlling parent?
Are you devoting too much attention to your child?
If the answer is yes,
then turn some of that attention toward your parents.
If you are good to your own parents,
then your child will learn how to treat
you in the future.

From a young age,
some children are told to compete,
worried about what their parents will say,
insecure about how their friends will judge them.

Let them know it is okay to enjoy life.
Help them discover talents that cannot be graded.
Respect them so they know what it feels like
to be respected.

Establish a goal for the week.
There is a big difference between having a goal and not having one.
A significant accomplishment can be traced back to a single thought.

✳

Even if you have just a modest dream,
don't keep it to yourself. Talk to others about it.
By the time you tell ten people, it is more likely to come true.

✳

Try these two things at the same time:
Pretend you are already a champion
and work diligently at becoming one.
The gap between belief and reality will soon close.

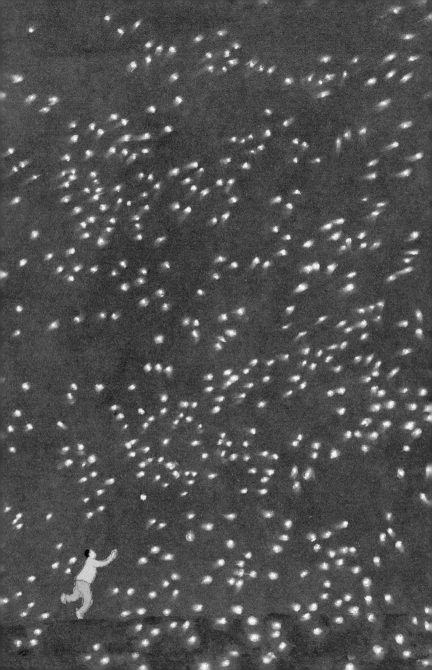

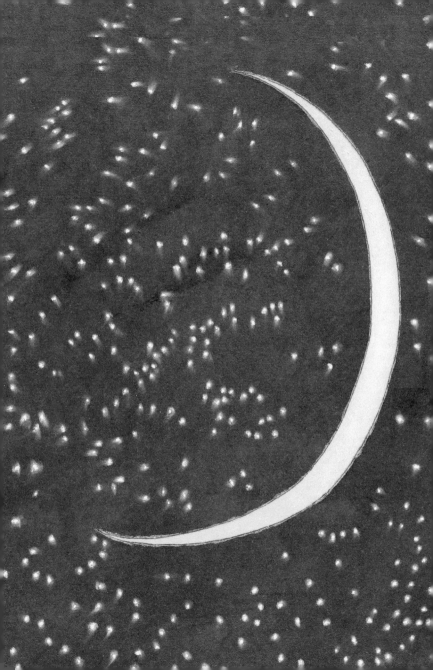

When You Look for Your Calling

It is not easy to find one's calling in life. Although some know what they want to do from an early age, for most, it takes many years to find their path. Whenever I am asked about finding one's calling, I offer the following advice.

First, one of the reasons it is difficult to find your calling is that you simply do not know what kind of jobs are out there in the world. Where can you discover options other than the jobs you already know of through your family and friends?

The easiest way to expose yourself to an array of indirect experiences is by reading. Have you read up on science, travel, fashion, art, or politics? How about education, psychology, finance, health, food, music, or sports? Read widely as you explore different professions. You can also read a biography of someone you admire and hope to emulate. Books broaden your horizons and introduce you to new possibilities.

Second, it is hard to find one's calling because many mistakenly believe they need to look only within to discover their passion. Although it is true that we have innate interests and talents, we often do not know what they are until we have real-life experiences. Having a wide range of experiences can help you uncover your inner passion.

Try various part-time jobs and internships, or volunteer.

Don't be afraid of rolling up your sleeves and diving in.

While immersed in a job's reality, you will discover whether it's a good fit.

Work experiences may unlock the door to a career opportunity you hadn't considered.

Third, it is difficult to find your calling without sufficient self-awareness. Do you know what kind of work environment you thrive in? Do you draw your energy from interacting with people? Do you perform well under pressure? What are your strengths and weaknesses?

You can increase your self-awareness by interacting with a wide range of people in a wide variety of situations. You will develop a deeper understanding of yourself as you cultivate relationships, which become a mirror reflecting your strengths and weaknesses in various circumstances. Do not be afraid of meeting new people. Get to know those who are working in a field you are interested in. Go out on dates; they are another good way to learn about yourself. Discover what

types of people are compatible with your personality. From these experiences, you will gain insight into what kinds of people you like to surround yourself with.

Lastly, do not select your career based on what others will think of your choice. The truth is that other people do not really think about you that much. If you think you will enjoy something, then do not overthink it. Just do it. Even if it does not turn out the way you imagined it, you will still appreciate it for what it has taught you.

I wish you the best of luck!

Measure your self-worth
not with the balance of your bank account
but with the frequency of your generosity.

✻

The college you graduated from is not that important.
The life you have chosen to live after college is.

✻

"When hiring, I like people who are confident but who
can admit when they are wrong.
For that kind of person, I don't have to look at any
other credentials,
because they are sure of themselves but won't let their
ego get in the way."
—AHN CHEOL-SOO,
SOUTH KOREAN SOFTWARE ENTREPRENEUR

When you look for a job,
try to find out how long a company's employees stay at
the company.
This is more important than the size of the company
or the salary offered.
If people keep leaving, then that says a lot.

✳

Are you nervous or even terrified about your new job?
Is it because you are afraid of disappointing your new
boss?
Just do the best you can without being self-conscious
about your work.
Even if your work is less than superb, if you are sincere
and dedicated,
then your boss and colleagues will appreciate you.

If you happen to visit a workplace that appears much
better than yours,
instead of feeling envious, examine the place
more carefully.
You may find a downside that changes your first
impression.
The moment you realize that, you will feel grateful for
your current job.

*

Being a good boss requires much more than
just having a lot of technical knowledge.
It is important to have integrity and a positive
relationship with the staff,
to give timely feedback and professional
mentoring, and
to advocate for what the team needs.

A boss should not be overly concerned with
how she is perceived.
This is secondary.
Rather, she should focus on how her work affects
the staff and clients.

✳

A wise leader doesn't assemble a team of only those
who agree with him.
He needs someone who disagrees with him,
to allow him to see his blind spots.

✳

An inept leader attempts to micromanage everything.
His staff will wind up doing only what they are told.
A skillful leader knows how to delegate
to subordinates
and to wait for them to take responsibility and see
the job to a successful conclusion.

Dedication to one's job should not be measured
by how late one works
or how often one forgoes a vacation
but by how effectively one works and
what kind of contribution one makes to the business.

✳

People often have unrealistic expectations
of the success of their first book, album, or show.
Just as there is no effect without a cause,
success doesn't come about by luck alone,
without years of preparation and hard work.

✳

It is not always a good thing to get what you want.
If everything happens the way you want,
it is easy to become lazy and arrogant.
You may also lose the ability to empathize with people
having difficulties.
Perhaps any hardship you may experience is an
important life lesson.

Long-Lost Cousins

Do not judge so that you will not be judged.
For in the way you judge, you will be judged;
and by your stand of measure, it will be measured to you.
—MATTHEW 7:1–2

WHENEVER I READ the above biblical passage, I am reminded of a similar philosophy in the Buddhist tradition called the law of karma. As many people know, it is the law of cause and effect often described succinctly in the West as, "You reap what you sow," or "What goes around comes around." It is a wonderful admonition that compels us to examine the consequences of our thought, speech, and behavior. Although I am a Buddhist, I have been deeply influenced by many passages in the Bible. The first time I picked up the Bible for serious study was in college, for my comparative religion class. I learned about the history of Christianity and analyzed various biblical lessons, and soon I began to open my heart to it. I realized that Truth is not the exclusive property of any one religion. It has a universal quality that allows people of different religious traditions to recognize and respect it.

About two years ago I had the unique opportunity to visit a rural French village called Taizé, in eastern Burgundy, along with elder monks from my Buddhist order. It is an ecumenical Christian monastic community, where monastic brothers live according to the Bible. Taizé is famous as a Christian pilgrimage site, each year attracting more than a hundred thousand young adults from all over the world. The pilgrims usually spend several days in the community while participating in morning, midday, and evening prayers as well as quiet reflection and small group discussions. I was already familiar with the Taizé community's soul-stirring chants and was looking forward to attending their wonderful prayer service.

When we arrived at beautiful Taizé, the brothers came

out and greeted us warmly. Clad in white robes, they had gentle smiles and a peaceful presence, almost as if they were angels incarnated. Our light gray monastic robes looked quite similar to their white ones, and it was as if we had become one large family. The brothers gave us a tour of the community and, to officially welcome us, chanted "Confitemini Domino"—one of the most beautiful songs I've heard in my life. We were invited to their living quarters and had a nice chat followed by midday prayers in the Church of Reconciliation. The more time we spent in Taizé, the more I could see the similarities to Buddhist monastic living. The brothers spent hours in silent prayer as a way to turn their attention to God within, not unlike our silent meditation practice. Another similarity was that the brothers wore a ring to signify their vows to God; monks from my order "wear" a small incense burn on our left arm when we receive our full precepts.

Some may think that life in such a community is repressed, strict, and difficult, but that is not the case. A monastic life is characterized by simple beauty and unexpected joy. Monks find happiness in things that may seem trivial to those who pursue the material trappings of success. Watching the seasons change—the blossoming of the magnolias, the dazzling fall foliage, the first snowfall—brings indescribable joy and gratitude. A simple meal made with fresh ingredients from the nearby mountains is a source of great contentment. Because our monastic brothers are our friends, teachers, and family, we are never lonely.

At lunch we were presented, to our complete surprise, with kimchi. We were told that the brothers had gathered a few days before our arrival to make it themselves. We were so moved by their hospitality and did not know how to reciprocate. Although we were from a different religion and country, they welcomed us with consideration and love. When we left Taizé, we felt as though we'd just visited our long-lost cousins. I knew I would cherish this bond for the rest of my life. Even now, when I see one of the elder monks who visited Taizé with me, we fondly recall eating the brothers' kimchi with baguettes.

"How should we consider a different spiritual path?
We shall approach it with humility
as well as a willingness to learn about
another tradition.
If our faith can be shaken
from merely learning about a different tradition,
then that faith is not worth keeping."
—REVEREND DR. KANG WON YONG (1917–2006)

*

Just as my faith is precious and significant to me,
wouldn't it be the same for people of other faiths?
Just as my mother is dear and important to me,
wouldn't this be the case for my neighbor
and his mother?

May people know how to differentiate between
the certainty of one's faith and the folly of attacking
other faiths.
May faith never become an ideological weapon
to justify violence.

*

If Jesus, Buddha, and Confucius were all alive and
gathered in the same place,
would they argue over who is right?
Or would they respect and admire one another's
teachings?
Religious conflict can often be blamed
not on the founders of religions
but on their fanatical followers.

"The purpose of religion is to control yourself,
not to criticize others.
How much am I doing about my anger, attachment,
hatred, pride, and jealousy?
These are the things we must check in our daily lives."
—HIS HOLINESS, THE DALAI LAMA

*

If the essence is forgotten, ritual takes over.
When ritual dominates spiritual practice,
our outward appearances become more important than
our inner experience.
For instance, if you meditate in the hope of enlightenment,
how long and with whom you meditate
is not as important as
how your practice has changed your heart and your
relationships.

According to Professor Kang-Nam Oh,
the faithful can be divided roughly into two groups:
people of "surface faith" and people
of "in-depth faith."
The surface faithful are bound by spiritual symbols;
they often dispute the spiritual symbols of other faiths.
The in-depth faithful understand meanings deeper
than the symbols.
They can find similar meanings in the symbolism
of diverse spiritual traditions,
and harmony among such traditions.

*

"Heretic" is a loaded term.
It has been slapped on any belief or practice
that doesn't conform to the dominant
spiritual belief of an era.
If you are calling a spiritual path heretical,
remember that
yours was once considered as such when it first started.

"He who knows only one religion knows none."
—MAX MÜLLER (1823–1900),
GERMAN SCHOLAR OF COMPARATIVE
LANGUAGE, RELIGION, AND MYTHOLOGY

✳

Ignorance of other spiritual paths combined with fear
can give rise to religious persecution and violence.
Major wisdom traditions around the world teach
humility, love, and forbearance.
Nothing bad will come of learning about them.

✳

You can admire a spiritual leader but
never idolize him.
Blind faith in the leader can easily reduce you
to acting like a child,
handing over your power and asking the leader
to do things for you.
Medicine can be prescribed, but it must be
you who takes it.

A spiritual leader is a finger pointing at the moon.
If the finger attempts to become the moon,
this can lead to a grave sin.

＊

We must cultivate all three intelligences
for our overall health:
critical intelligence, emotional intelligence,
and spiritual intelligence.
If one falls to the wayside, it slows the growth
of the other two.

If you have developed critical intelligence but neglected emotional intelligence,
then you may not be sensitive to the suffering of others.
If you have developed emotional intelligence but neglected spiritual intelligence,
then you may lose hope after seeing the world's suffering.
If you have developed spiritual intelligence but neglected critical intelligence,
then you may fall victim to the abuse of a cult.

Whatever the circumstances, do not feel inferior.
Remember that God has created you in His divine
image.
You are the most precious daughter or son of God.
You are also the Buddha, even if you have
not realized it yet.
You have the same Buddha nature as all buddhas in the
universe.
Do not allow anyone to make you feel less than that.

Faith is overvalued while practice is undervalued.
If we emphasize faith over practice,
spirituality remains ideology, creating theological
conflicts.
But if we focus on carrying out the teachings in our
actual lives,
we realize that the love taught by Jesus
is no different from the compassion taught by the
Buddha.
If you wish for peace among different spiritual paths,
then practice what you preach.

*

Three Bible verses I cherish:

"In everything, therefore, treat people the same way
you want them to treat you,
for this is the Law and the Prophets."
—MATTHEW 7:12

"Not everyone who says to Me, 'Lord, Lord,' will enter
the kingdom of heaven,
but he who does the will of My Father who is in
heaven will enter."
—MATTHEW 7:21

"Truly I say to you, to the extent that you did it to one
of these brothers of Mine,
even the least of them, you did it to Me."
—MATTHEW 25:40

Two Spiritual Paths in One Family

When your spiritual path is different from that of your fiancé, when your siblings try to convert you to their new faith, when your child decides to follow a different path, this can create tension, awkwardness, and stress. Disagreements and arguments can erupt, and all of a sudden you find yourself negotiating how to carry out a funeral, wedding, religious holiday.

It is ironic that spirituality can become a source of conflict when its teachings are often about love and reconciliation. For those having problems with two spiritual paths in one family, I would like to offer this advice.

Above all, please understand that what makes you feel tense and awkward is not the spirituality itself but the pressure from your family to conform. You may resent their coerciveness and self-righteousness. You may feel their spiritual path is strange and unorthodox.

A good remedy to a situation like this is to learn more about the other spiritual path. Find a book by a respected member of that path and study it. If you are open-minded and willing to learn, then you will soon discover some aspects of that path resonating with yours. Although the outer spiritual symbols are different, the meaning behind them may sound oddly familiar to you.

You can also read a biography of a great spiritual teacher in that tradition, such as Mahatma Gandhi, Martin Luther King Jr., Mother Teresa, or the Dalai Lama. As you learn more about their lives and faiths, you will be able to appreciate their courage and come to respect their path. This change of attitude will positively influence the family dynamic. Although you cannot control how your family feels about your path, at least you will no longer feel uneasy about theirs.

But if your family continues to be narrow-minded and to show disrespect, then speak up confidently and educate them. Tell them the great leaders of their path did not act that way. Martin Luther King Jr. and Thich Nhat Hanh respected each other; Thomas Merton and the Dalai Lama were good friends.

Those who understand deeper meanings beyond the surface and who try to embody humility and peace also recognize the familiar inner light flickering in the eyes of other religious followers.

When this happens, they become more humble and open to the mysteries of human incarnation while feeling connected to the fragility of human hearts.

We don't receive more love from God by asking for it.
Rather, we awaken to the truth that God has always
loved us unconditionally.
We don't turn into a buddha by striving for it.
Rather, we awaken to the truth that we have been
buddhas all along.

❉

In the beginning, our prayer takes the shape of,
"Please grant me this, please grant me that,"
and then develops into, "Thank you for everything,"
and then matures into, "I want to resemble you."
Eventually it transcends language,
and we pray with our whole being in sacred silence.

As my prayer deepens,
I hear more of His voice than my words.
As my humility grows,
I feel more of His love overflowing in my heart.
As my mind quiets down,
I sense more of His presence in every moment.

✳

As your faith and spiritual practice deepen,
the sense of a separate self or ego diminishes,
leaving more room for divinity to fill your heart.
If you have prayed mostly to benefit yourself,
then shift gears and try praying to give up some of
your control.

If you have been praying like this—
"Please grant me this. I really need this to happen"—
then try to pray this way as well—
"Enlarge my heart to hold and accept the things
I cannot."
Do not bargain with God, Buddha, or any divine being
to give you what you want in exchange for material
offerings.

*

If you do not know how to solve a problem in your life,
give prayer a try.
As you bring your attention inward and sincerely seek
an answer,
something sacred within you unlocks the door of inner
wisdom.

If you are desperately looking to meet someone special,
send your prayer out to the universe.
The universe is an amazing matchmaker.

✳

Monastics can pray for many years because
their prayers of happiness for others make them happy.
As I prepare to officiate at my friend's wedding,
I become joyous.

✳

For unenlightened people, not every day is a good day,
because they feel happy only when things happen the
way they want them to.
For enlightened people, every single day is a good day,
because they feel free knowing that nothing can take
away their wisdom.

When an unenlightened person does good, he tries to
leave his mark.
When an enlightened person does good,
he leaves no marks.

❋

The holier a person is,
the more likely it is that she describes herself
as a sinner.
This is because she doesn't lie to herself.

❋

"The saints are what they are
not because their sanctity makes them admirable
to others
but because the gift of sainthood makes it possible for
them to admire everybody else."
—THOMAS MERTON*

*Thomas Merton, *New Seeds of Contemplation* (New York: New Directions, 2007).

Clergy and teachers tend to be verbose,
and older clergy and teachers even more so.
I hope I don't become that person who talks endlessly
without noticing how the person in front of me feels.

※

It is a sign of great spiritual strength
to keep someone else's secret.

※

"When a minister preaches, he must preach
not only to the congregation but also to himself."
—Reverend Hong Jeong-gil

According to Cardinal Nicolas Cheong Jin-suk,
"There is no record of the biblical story of one fish
multiplying to two or three.
There is also no record of fish falling from the sky.
What probably happened was that people took out
their lunches
and shared their food with others after listening to
Jesus' moving prayer."
A miracle is not just an otherworldly phenomenon
transcending the laws of nature.
Letting go of self-centeredness and opening one's heart
to others
are just as miraculous.

There is a simple way to test the veracity of the
Buddha's teachings.
Find the most comfortable posture.
Remain in that posture for thirty minutes.
The most comfortable posture soon becomes the most
uncomfortable.
Everything is impermanent, including the world's most
comfortable posture.

✳

Do not force yourself on a spiritual path.
Let its teachings gently open your heart and lead you.
Like salt gradually dissolving in water, let the teachings
dissolve in your heart.

Your Original Face

When you are so busy that you feel perpetually chased, when worrying thoughts circle your head, when the future seems dark and uncertain, when you are hurt by what someone has said, slow down, even if only for a moment. Bring all of your awareness into the present and take a deep breath.

What do you hear? What does your body feel? What does the sky look like?

Only when we slow down can we finally see clearly our relationships, our thoughts, our pain. As we slow down, we are no longer tangled in them. We can step out and appreciate them for what they are.

The faces of our family and colleagues who always help, the scenery that we pass by every day but fail to notice, our friends' stories that we fail to pay attention to—in the stillness of the pause, the entirety of our being is quietly revealed.

Wisdom is not something we have to strive to acquire. Rather, it arises naturally as we slow down and notice what is already there.

As we notice more and more in the present moment, we come to a deeper realization that a silent observer is within us. In the primordial stillness, the silent observer witnesses everything inside and outside.

Befriend the silent observer. Find out where it is, and what shape it has assumed. Do not try to imagine it as something you already know. Let all your thoughts and images merge back into silence and just sense the observer already there in silence.

If you see the face of the silent observer, then you have found your original face, from before you were born.